This book has been published with the kind support of the
East German Savings Bank Foundation in the Free State of Saxony,
together with the Saxon Savings Banks.

Saxony's Finest Palaces, Castles and Gardens

Sachsens Schönste Schlösser, Burgen und Gärten

Edition Leipzig

Frontispiece: Dresdner Zwinger –
A view of the Mathematical Physical Salon

www.schloesser-sachsen.de
www.edition-leipzig.de

Text: Reinhard Delau, Dresden
Translated from the German by Paul Bewicke, Hamburg
Cover and layout: Atelier für grafische Gestaltung, Leipzig
English Edition: Berliner Buchwerkstatt, Kate Hughes and Britta Dieterle
Reproduction: Förster & Borries GmbH, Zwickau
Printing and Binding: Westermann Druck Zwickau GmbH, Zwickau
Printed in Germany

ISBN: 3-361-00576-0

Printed on age-resitant paper with chlorine-free bleached cellulose.

Table of Contents

Dresdner Zwinger

One of »the world's finest pleasure-gardens« – Dresdner Zwinger

»The Zwinger has become a symbol for Dresden,« the art historian Fritz Löffler wrote. Its beginnings were somewhat unusual. In the Baroque era, it became customary for rulers to keep at their courts exotic plants and trees brought from southern climes. Elector Friedrich August I of Saxony, being a true child of his time, shared this passion and avidly ordered lemon, orange and pomegranate trees to be procured. Inconveniently, his royal residence did not have adequate winter quarters, so for years he was forced to shelter some of his exotic plants with a wealthy Leipzig businessman by the name of Apel. The Elector was not prepared to put up with this situation any longer, especially as other rulers' residences boasted fine orangeries, and he did not want to appear inferior.

In 1709, Friedrich August I decided to build an orangerie. It was to be erected in the Zwinger gardens close to the palace. To design it, he chose Matthäus Daniel Pöppelmann of Herford, who responded by producing his greatest work of architecture, the Zwinger. The first payment was remitted »for our acquired and still growing orangerie.« By a happy coincidence, client and architect got on well and demanded high standards of each other. They were soon joined by a third man, sculptor Balthasar Permoser, who hailed from Bavaria. Dresden was fortunate in having two gifted residents capable of fashioning sandstone into light-hearted, festive architecture.

The Zwinger building work ran into difficulties. Pöppelmann had grandiose plans. His idea was to design for the Elector a »Garden of the Hesperides,« a complex stretching down to the River Elbe, complete with terraces, gardens and buildings. Pöppelmann's design broke through the town for-

Page 7:
The Ramparts Pavilion

Crown Gate and courtyard side of the Long Galleries

The Semper Gallery

1709 The King of Denmark visits Dresden. A wooden building is erected for the court society opposite the palace as a festival ground for tournaments, games, functions, fairs, etc. It is demolished in 1714, and Augustus the Strong commissions Matthäus Daniel Pöppelmann to build an orangerie to house his collection of rare Mediterranean plants (Ramparts Pavilion, Mathematical-Physical Salon, French Pavilion with arched galleries and Nymphs' Pool).

tifications, with the result that it was staunchly opposed by the military. Dresden was surrounded by a wall and ramparts and anyone who breached them was endangering the town's security. The city's ability to defend itself was more important than architectural ambitions. The military officers turned down Pöppelmann's plans. The Elector fell into a quandary. Who should he listen to, whose side should he take? On one hand was the city's security, on the table Pöppelmann's drawings disregarding ramparts and wall. The state architect and master builder had grown bold. Pöppelmann wanted to build the Elector a long gallery and a gate topped by an intricate crown on parts of the fortification wall. The death of

Emperor Joseph in Vienna furthered the building project. Until a new Emperor was elected, Augustus the Strong was in charge of imperial business. His elation with this new abundance of power – he even dreamed of becoming emperor – led to victory for the architect. The Elector decreed that room was to be made for his plans. Pöppelmann's Zwinger forced the city to be opened a little, while the Baroque building style ensured wide open spaces. The Elector, who was also King of Poland, must have been highly satisfied with his architect, for he sent him to Vienna, Paris and Versailles to study architecture there. The Nymphs' Pool cascades were begun in around 1715, as was the Mathematical and Physical Salon. These were followed by the French Pavilion, and the long galleries and the Crown Gate were also under way.

On his return from France, Pöppelmann was brimming with creative energy. He was keen to put his perceptions and ideas into practice in the Zwinger. By his side he had Permoser, a sculptor who was his equal. In their hands, the architectural work of art began to take shape despite repeated shortages of money. A second event of European significance came to the aid of the Zwinger's creators. In 1718 the Elector's heir, the future Elector Friedrich August II, was betrothed to Maria Josepha, daughter of the Emperor of Austria. The Elector needed a suitably imposing festival ground for the grand wedding celebrations to be held in Dresden in 1719. Pöppelmann came up with the idea of building a mirror image of the buildings by the ramparts on the side facing the town. This must surely have been Pöppelmann's happiest period. The Elector pressed for the work to proceed quickly, and Pöppelmann was only too happy to oblige. He had experienced Augustus the Strong's changes of mind too often, the way in which the Elector turned his interest to other buildings or rejected what had previously been decided.

1710–1712 The long gallery by the ramparts pavilion is built.

1711 The orangerie project is extended: a garden is designed and building work on the Nymphs' Pool is started.

1712–1716 The Mathematical-Physical Salon and the French Pavilion are built, with ceiling paintings by Louis de Silvestre and Heinrich Christian Fehling (1717–1723).

1714–1718 The Crown Gate and long galleries with sculpture by Balthasar Permoser are built.

1716–1719 Building of the Ramparts Pavilion.

1718/19 Southern pavilion buildings and a wooden interim building are built on the Elbe side.

1719 The Zwinger is formally opened with a function to mark the wedding of Electoral Prince Friedrich August to Archduchess Maria Josepha. This type of festivity, with the royal couple playing landlord and landlady and the nobility turning up in all manner of costumes, was already very popular in Saxony at the time of Elector Augustus.

1728 The Zwinger buildings are completed and used to house collections and a library. The statues adorning the Zwinger are by Permoser.

Since 1728 The most valuable Dresden collections have been housed in the Zwinger.

1746 The Mathematical-Physical Salon is established on its present site.

1759/60 Damaged in the Seven Years War. The Zwinger is used by the Prussian army as a store and living quarters.

1783–1795 First Zwinger restoration under the supervision of Johann Daniel Schade.

1806–1813 The Zwinger suffers damage during the Napoleonic Wars. The moat is filled in (the town is de-fortified).

1820–1830 The Zwinger lake and garden in the Zwinger courtyard are laid out, together with the pools.

1847–1855 The Elbe side is completed with the gallery building designed by Gottfried Semper, with sculptural ornamentation by Ernst Rietschel.

1849 Following popular unrest in May, the opera house burns down. The Zwinger's southern pavilion and town-side pavilion suffer extensive damage.

1857–1863 Reconstruction and second restoration under the supervision of Karl Moritz Haenel.

1880–1898 Third restoration, including repairs to the structure (using Portland cement, iron cramps and oil paint).

1924–1936 Founding of the Zwinger Bauhütte, or guild, headed by Hubert Ermisch. This is followed by thorough measures to make the building safe, and a fourth, comprehensive restoration.

1945 Air-raids totally destroy the Zwinger.

As the wedding festivities drew near, the triad of buildings on the town side was still unfinished. Wooden buildings closed the gaps. Wooden stands were erected along the side where Gottfried Semper later built his art gallery. After the wedding, a difficult period began for progress with the Zwinger. The coffers were empty and the Elector was in debt. The year 1720 passed by without any further work being done to the Zwinger. No funds were approved in 1721 either. Pöppelmann's attempts to persuade the Elector to resume building were in vain. The Zwinger was in danger of remaining a fragment until finally, in 1723, the Elector approved

The Nymphs' Pool

some funds. Money continued to flow in the years that followed, sparsely but regularly. Pöppelmann was able to proceed with his work. By 1728 he had completed the Zwinger in its present form. In 1729, Pöppelmann was 67 and must have suspected that his idea of continuing the complex down to the Elbe could no longer be accomplished. The Elector had long turned his attention to other buildings. Pöppelmann ordered a copper etching to be made of his masterpiece, entitled »L'Orangerie Royale de Dresde.«

What Pöppelmann had feared, came to pass. The Zwinger was never extended down to the Elbe. The Elector lost interest in the building, which was used only a few times for festivities. In Augustus the Strong's lifetime, the pavilions and galleries were put to use in a way that nobody had previously hit upon. In 1728 the Elector had art collections placed in the Zwinger because he could not afford a new museum. Noteworthy collections are still displayed in the pavilions and salons, including mathematical and physical equipment, globes of the Earth and celestial globes, world maps and atlases, valuable porcelain from Meißen and the Far East. Contemporary taste dictated that members of later generations should find the Zwinger, and Baroque architecture as a whole, unattractive. The classicist architect Karl Friedrich Schinkel noted in 1803 in Dresden: »Zwinger, extensive building made of square stones, surrounds a large, quadrangular public area. Full of an astonishing array of shells and flowers in the worst style.« Calling to mind the festive architecture that is part of Dresden's Baroque splendour, the leading literary expert Hermann Hettner wrote with great empathy: »Like the fashionable dance of its day, the minuet, it (the Zwinger) is the measured, light-hearted animation of coquettish grace, a summer night's dream in the style of Versailles.«

Pavilion with chiming bells

1945–1963 Reconstruction under the supervision of Hubert Ermisch, Arthur Frenzel and Max Zimmermann.

1952 The first exhibition room is reopened.

1985 Start of total restoration.

1991 The Zwinger guild is refounded.

1993 The Zwinger becomes part of the newly established Dresden state castles and gardens administration.

A traveller's tale, 1856

In the summer months the famous royal orangerie is set up in the middle of the Zwinger. It consists of 300 trees, some of which owe their origin to a natural history journey to North Africa undertaken 100 years ago by two Leipzig professors at the behest of Friedrich August II. The travellers brought back as ballast a number of orange trees for the king's woodturning lathe, and attempts were made to get them to shoot and in many cases, after great effort, succeeded.

The Zwinger interior is a superb sight with its green lawns, fountains, fine buildings, the king's statue and the large orangerie, enlivened by countless groups of children and strollers seen from the centre looking out and, especially, looking down from the Zwinger ramparts in the outer grounds at the back of the west side adjacent to the great pavilion. Since last year the eye has rested with pleasure on the imposing facade of the new museum occupying the fourth, north side of the Zwinger where there was previously no building, but only a bare boundary wall.

From: Menchen, G.: Romantische Reise durch Sachsen, reprinted 1987, p. 167

Dresdner Stallhof

A touch of Italy in Dresden

Dresden's historic town centre, between the Georgenbau (George's Building) and the Jüdenhof (Jews' Yard), boasts a rare attraction – the »kurfürstlicher Reissige Stall« (electoral knights' stables) with the Stallhof, or Stable Courtyard, and the Langer Gang, or Long Walk. The foundation stone for this complex of buildings was laid in 1586. The buildings are one of the few pieces of remaining testimony to Dresden Renaissance architecture. But what architectural testimony! Twenty-two Tuscan pillars support the Long Walk's airy arches, covering a long arcade. The facades are decorated with sgraffiti, white and grey patterns etched into the plaster. A sun dial measures the time. And at the back of the Long Walk, on the wall facing Augustusstrasse, a long procession of rulers rides on horseback. They are the Wettins, the dynasty that ruled the margravate of Meißen and Saxony as margraves, dukes, electors and kings until the November Revolution of 1918. Inside the Stable Courtyard where knights and retainers demonstrated their jousting and coursing skills, two bronze columns have been preserved in their original state. They once held the rings which the participants tried to lift as they galloped past.

In the Stable Courtyard and under the arcades one senses a breath of Italy. Along with the German architect and builder Hans Irmisch, it is thought to have been the Italian Giovanni Maria Nosseni who left the mark of Mediterranean light-heartedness in the Dresden stones. When the Albertinian line of Wettins chose Dresden to be its permanent royal seat, the town was still overshadowed by Freiberg, Meißen, Pirna and Wittenberg. But along with Duke George the Bearded came the new architectural style from the South, which the majority of Gothic masters resisted. The Duke built himself a monument in the shape of the first Georgenbau, which unfortuna-

Page 15: The Stallhof and, behind it, the tower of the Hofkirche

The »Long Walk« with its Tuscan pillars

tely disappeared in the smoke of time. After that, there was no holding back the new architectural style in Dresden. Mediaeval Dresden saw its first major period of construction. Moritz, the Albertinian Elector who moved his capital from Wittenberg to Dresden, a temporary ally of Emperor Charles V and victor of Mühlberg, wanted to see his status elevated in a new palace. He issued orders for the old Dresden palace to be altered and extended into a magnificent four-winged complex. The townspeople followed suit and adorned their houses with bay windows and ornate facades. Dresden rose to become a leading German Renaissance town. Hardly any of it survived the centuries. Nearly 150 years later Friedrich August I, better known as Augustus the Strong, came to power. He developed

1565–1567 During the reign of Elector Augustus, building of the Kanzleihaus, or chancellery, by Hans Irmisch, with frescos by Benedetto da Tola.

1586–1588 Paul Buchner lays out a racecourse in front of the palace's south-east corner.

1586–1591 The entire complex is built under the guidance of Buchner and Irmisch. Three-winged building (two storeys), enclosed courtyard and a spiral staircase in each corner of the yard, »Long Walk« with 22 round-arched arcades open on the

The Princes' Procession (part)

courtyard side, probably designed by Giovanni Maria Nosseni, long hall for the Wettins' ancestors gallery, later the rifle gallery (until 1945), the »Kurfürstlicher Reissige Stall« with stable courtyard by the old outer town wall, to accommodate carriages and horses on the ground floor, the armoury and noble guests on the upper floor, graffiti by Heinrich Göding in the yard: two bronze columns for ring jousting, cast by Martin Hilger in 1601 from designs by Nosseni.

1722–1725 First conversion works under the guidance of architect Johann Georg Maximilian von Fürstenhoff.

1744–1746 Second redesign under Johann Christoph Knöffel (horses' watering-place, gallery building). Until the mid-18th

a great passion for building, clearing aside any buildings from a previous era that got in his way. Breaking rigorously with the previous architectural era, he had buildings designed in the new Baroque style, a style that was thereafter to shape the city. The Stable Courtyard and Long Walk survived unscathed, and remain to convey an impression of Renaissance architecture in Dresden, a style which is now so rare.

It is worth noting how functional buildings provide testimony to major architecture. Initially, the »kurfürstlicher Reissige Stall,« later the Johanneum and now a transport museum, was designed to accommodate the court's horses and carriages. But the palace's vicinity meant the complex had to be suitably imposing. On the upper floor, the Wettin rulers showed off their armouries, and people who were sufficiently upper-class and had enough blue blood in their veins were allowed to stay there. What is more, the area became an island of art. The Long Walk's elongated hall held portraits of Wettin ancestors in valuable frames, and later a rifle gallery.

And after conversion, Dresden used the stable building to show the world its valuable collection of paintings. The collection acquired European status especially in the reign of Friedrich August II, son of Augustus the Strong. Johann Wolfgang von Goethe, who visited Dresden as a student, described the gallery in his work »Dichtung und Wahrheit« as a »holy place.« »I entered this holy place and my astonishment was greater than anything I had imagined.« The paintings remained until Gottfried Semper built the art gallery on the Theaterplatz.

After being destroyed in 1945, the Stable Courtyard and Long Walk have been restored to their original beauty. Connoisseurs say the complex is the only one of its kind in the world. The Stable Courtyard, originally designed as a tournament and festival ground for the court and nobility, is thought to be the only one that has been preserved, at least in Germany. The man to whom Dresden owes this architectural monument is preserved for eternity in the »Princes' Procession.« He was Elector Christian I. Well may one look up in gratitude at his picture, along with those of his fellow-Wettins, portrayed in Meißen porcelain tiles. The Stable Courtyard, stable building and Long Walk are his finest bequest.

century: venue for court amusements such as tournaments, ring jousting, coursing, fox-beating.

1794–1857 Houses the Mengsisches Museum, further use as a stable.

1872–1877 Last conversion under Carl Moritz Haenel, called the Johanneum. The armoury collection, Germany's largest and most important collection of weapons, is put on show in what is now the Historical Museum.

1935 Restored to its original condition.

1945 Suffers destruction during the bombing of Dresden.

From 1950 The complex is reconstructed.

1956 The Transport Museum is opened in the Johanneum.

1972–1979 The ensemble undergoes extensive reconstruction.

1993 The Stallhof becomes part of the newly founded Dresden castles and gardens administration.

From the Dresden Princes' Procession

Friedrich der Freidige und Gebissene
Margrave of Meißen
Ruled 1307–1323

Friedrich I, Margrave of Meißen, had two nicknames, »der Freidige,« meaning »the Bold,« and »der Gebissene,« meaning »the Bitten.« The latter can be taken completely literally, even if the following episode is not historically proven.

When Friedrich's mother Margareta (a daughter of Emperor Friedrich II) left her unfaithful husband Margrave Albrecht II on the Wartburg in 1270, she bade an affectionate farewell to her beloved son, who was 13 at the time. Bemoaning her fate, she kissed him passionately and ended up biting the unsuspecting boy on the cheek, thus marking him for ever.

Cf. Nadolski, D.: Wahre Geschichte um den Dresdner Fürstenzug. Taucha, 1993, p. 22; and Zimmermann, I.: Sachsens Markgrafen, Kurfürsten und Könige. Berlin, 1990. S. 51 f.

Brühlsche Terrasse in Dresden

Dresden's finest balcony rests on the darkness of a fortress

The Brühlsche Terrasse is Dresden's finest balcony. From it, one sees the city from its brightest side. The Elbe valley with its hills, the spacious meadows and the river separating the old and new towns. Close to its banks, majestic buildings define the city: Gottfried Semper's opera house and the art gallery on the Theaterplatz, and on the right bank two ministries which, in the days when they were built in the Neustadt, symbolised the bourgeois way of life, in contrast to the Wettins' centre of power, the palace. The Brühlsche Terrasse is the best vantage point for learning how talented architects handled the city and riverside space, turning the river into a festive street.

The former Catholic Hofkirche, or Court Church, now the cathedral of the episcopate of Dresden and Meißen, turns toward the Elbe as if in a grand movement. And the terrace itself abounds with lightness. It rises above the river bank as if it were purpose-built for admiring the view. Its history is exciting. It is more closely interwoven with the power and vanity of the man who had it built than perhaps any other place in Dresden. Two major phases of construction determined the balcony's history. The first, Baroque, phase, shaped by the enthusiastic builder and much-castigated minister Heinrich Graf von Brühl, has disappeared, the second can still be experienced.

A splendid painting done in 1747 by Bernardo Bellotto, who produced a chronicle of Dresden and its court in pictures, shows a view from the Brühlsche Terrasse. Elector Friedrich August II, Augustus the Strong's successor, gave permission for buildings to be erected on the site of the town fortifications, and gave some building land to Brühl as a present. Johann Christoph Knöffel became his preferred architect,

Page 21:
The Brühlsche Terrasse

constructing several buildings on the terrace: the art gallery, the library, the garden room and the Palais Brühl. All succumbed to the ravages of time or destruction or were rigorously demolished toward the end of the 19th century. All that remains is Brühl's garden and the former court plant and tree nursery, now a Reformed Church.

Walking up the sweeping open staircase towards clipped trees and a summery shade of yellow. At the bottom and top of the staircase Johannes Schilling's statues representing the times of day. On the right is the old Estates House (on the site of Brühl's palace) designed by Paul Wallot, architect of the Berlin Reichstag building. In front of it is the pool that was only uncovered and restored in 1989, then the delicately-proportioned Secundogenitur, the house of the Elector's second son (where the library used to be). For decades, this neo-Baroque building was a café, and has remained so as part of the Hilton Hotel. After that comes the mighty College of Fine Arts building and the Saxony Art Association's exhibition building (still a ruin), which is also owned by the Free State of Saxony. At the end of the terrace, a small park opens out. A dolphin fountain babbles in the shade of tall trees. The fountain and the park date back to Brühl's days. Some art historians regret the demolition of Brühl's buildings, and maybe they are right. For there disappeared along with them a type of architecture which served exclusively to elevate Brühl, his power and his artistic sense. He built more than his king, who had succumbed to collecting paintings. But where else was the late 19th century to show off its historic architecture? There was no space in the confinement of the historic city centre, so space was created by disrespectfully razing old buildings to the ground. Lipsius, the architect of the Art Academy, was the most extreme. His temple of art looks too massive, too showy, on its elevated site. Even so, the lightness

1519–1529 Fortifications built in Dresden in the rule of Duke George the Bearded (four bastions and first brick gate are built).

1545 Duke Moritz promulgates new building regulations for Dresden. These point out the necessity of renewing the fortifications. The Moritzmonument, produced in 1553 by Hans Walther, is erected by the eastern wall of the bastion in his memory.

By 1555 Dresden's fortifications are complete. Design and execution: Caspar Voigt von Wierandt.

1559–1563 A first armoury is built (since the 19th century it has been the Albertinum).

1589–1592 At Buchner's suggestion, a new bastion, the Jungfernbastei is built, as is the first belvedere (destroyed in 1747 after an explosion in the Vulkanshöhlen casemates).

1591/92 Construction of the casemates (in the rule of Augustus the Strong, known as the Vulkanshöhlen). The »New Dresden« fortress is completed.

1739 Count von Brühl has a palace and gardens built; the bastion courtyards are filled in.

1748–1751 The second belvedere, by Knöffel, is built (destroyed in 1759).

1814 Building of the flight of steps leading from Schlossplatz to the Brühlsche Terrasse, designed by Gottlob Friedrich Thormeyer.

1814 Building of the third belvedere designed by Christian Friedrich Schuricht, demolished in 1842. The Brühlsche Terrasse is opened to the public.

1828 Count von Brühl's garden pavilion is used as a Technical Education Institution.

1842 Building of the fourth belvedere by Otto von Wolframsdorf. Burned out on 13 February 1945 and later demolished.

1843 Building of the Café Reale by Otto von Wolframsdorf.

1868–1871 Erection of the four »times of the day« groups of figures by Johannes Schilling by the flight of steps up to the terrace.

1872 Count von Brühl's garden pavilion is demolished and the Rietschel monument (designed by Schilling) is erected.

1884–1900 The Brühlsche Terrasse is redesigned, the armoury is converted into the Albertinum, Knöffel's buildings are demolished. Building of the Kunstakademie and the art exhibition building.

1892 Erection of the monument to Gottfried Semper, by Schilling, by the Neuer Kunstverein building.

1895 The Moritz monument is installed on the Jungfernbastei.

1906 The Saxon state assembly building is completed.

1945 Air raids wreak destruction.

of this balcony, the view of river and hills have remained and inspire light-hearted feelings. Those who have soaked up enough of it can descend into the depths, into the darkness of the fortress upon which the balcony was built.

Beneath the Brühlsche Terrasse, they will find fortress vaults, a piece of Renaissance Dresden, a ramified network of battlemented parapets and gun courtyards. The building was opened to the public not very long ago. Thousands of cubic metres of rubble and infill had to be removed, walkways had to be installed, before the fortress could regularly accommodate the curious. Thanks is due to the efforts of tireless individuals who insisted that Dresden did not only boast Baroque architecture, and who wanted to demonstrate the fact. Immediately behind the fortress entrance on Georg-Treu-Platz is the Ziegeltor, or Brick Gate, »the last remaining town gate of the former royal seat.« It was closed roughly 400 years ago. Dark and damp, with giant vaults and stout walls, the small bastion with the cannon courtyard, casemates, marksmen's crenels and masons' signs left by the craftsmen. High-water marks record disasters to which the city was exposed. What a mighty defensive structure arose on the Elbe when Duke George and after him Elector Moritz issued the order to protect Dresden even better from attacks and sieges! In doing so, they were following the dictate of the times. People in Europe were afraid, especially of the Turks who were overrunning the old Occident. The stronger fortifications were to be capable of withstanding the new instruments of battle, heavy cannonballs.

The stones of the vaults gleam under electric lighting, arches support heavy loads. Dresden was once a major German Renaissance city. Hardly anything remained apart from the Stable Courtyard, two portals, the spiral-staircase towers in the Great Palace Courtyard, and the remains of the Jäger-

In the casemates

1990 Parts of the Renaissance vaults (casemates) are cleared of rubble and opened to visitors.

1993 The Brühlsche Terrasse is brought under the Dresden state castles and gardens administration.

hof hunting lodge. After 1808 the fortress walls that encircled old Dresden were demolished. Beneath the Brühlsche Terrasse, which turns its long fortress wall toward the Elbe, at least a piece of this impressive architectural history can still be seen. Indeed, since the fortress was opened, the Saxon capital has gained another major sightseeing attraction. One is tempted to toy with an idea: the lightness of the Brühlsche Terrasse rests on the darkness of a fortress. What a brilliant idea to build a city here.

Description of a Journey, 1823

All of Germany and half of Poland and Britain knows and praises and loves the Brühlsche Terrasse. The initial impression it made on me is renewed each time I see it. I associate it with the idea of a more southern lifestyle such as we northerners incessantly longed for from the beginning. This carefree hustle and bustle of a countless crowd that wants nothing but to enjoy the coolness of the river, the evening, the setting sun, the broad, open view, the strangers from every nation speaking in every language, the meetings with acquaintances one did not expect to find here, standing still and being torn away again – words cannot express how quickly and nimbly the threads of human existence become entwined here! What a bathing-resort sojourn offers over a series of days is formed here in just hours, indeed minutes, as the moments fleetingly glide by. Even without counting the large number of foreign residents in Dresden, the stream of spa visitors from nearly every Bohemian and Saxon watering-place passes through here like ebb and flow. Everyone wants to spend a few days recuperating in this delightful place, people try to find themselves a pretext for both prolonging and excusing their stay. The people who cross paths here in this way in the months of June, July and August! I would come to Dresden just for this one terrace alone!

De la Motte Fouqué, F., quoted in Menchen, G.:
Romantische Reise durch Sachsen. Leipzig. Reprinted 1987, p. 168

Großer Garten in Dresden

A melody of stone and nature – the Großer Garten

Happy the city that has such a garden. Entrances are lined with gateposts, sculptures stand on pedestals. All the flowers are in magnificent bloom. Narrow bridges span water-courses. Rowing boats bob up and down on the Carola Lake. A narrow-gauge engine sounds a warning whistle when the park railway crosses shady footpaths. And at the point where the avenues intersect stands a beautiful stone palace, casting its reflection on the surface of the lake in front. Hardly anything is heard of the roar of the noisy city. Here, in this flat landscape that once lay far outside the walls of the many-towered royal residence, Dresden's first Baroque palace was built as a summer palace for the Dresden court, for festivals and games.

Generations have shaped the Großer Garten, or Large Garden. Generations of princes and gardeners and architects. Toward the end of the 16th century, when the wall-fortified town became too small for the aristocracy and the court, pleasure-gardens appeared outside the city gates. There, the ladies and gentlemen could stroll and remember that there were other things in life apart from etiquette. The Elector ordered the first land purchases for the Großer Garten in 1676. Since then, each century has added something, the austerity of the geometrical French style, the Kavaliershäuser or Courtiers' Houses, the palace pond, an open-air theatre, sandstone and marble sculptures in dramatic poses, the sensitive reshaping into an English-style landscaped park, the little Carola palace and, more recently, from 1950, the park railway and the open-air and puppet theatre. For nearly one and a half centuries, the park was closed to ordinary people. That changed when the Russian general Prince Nikolai Repnin-Volkonsky came along. After the Battle of the Nations at Leipzig, in

*Page 27:
The Mosaic Fountain*

The palace and palace lake

1676 First garden plan by court gardener Martin Göttler. Start of the purchase of fields between Strehlen, Gruna and the outskirts of Pirna for a 700 x 700-cubit central area to form the Großer Garten's nucleus.

1677/78 The garden is extended in two stages to 1,700 x 1,700 cubits.

1678–1683 The palace is built under the supervision of Johann Georg Starcke. Situated at the intersection where the avenues meet, it is Dresden's first Baroque building and a major example of early German Baroque in general. The beginnings of the Renaissance-inspired garden planned by Göttler are completed.

From 1683 The gardens are extended and redesigned on the French model by Johann Friedrich Karcher. The Mailbahn (the present Hercules and South avenues) is laid out.

From 1684 Eight pavilions (courtiers' houses) are erected round the palace.

By 1687 Further land has been bought, bringing the total area to 3,300 x 3,300 cubits.

1688–1693 Return of some of the land and creation of the rectangular outline still visible today.

By 1719 The flower beds and groves around the palace have been created, along with the palace lake and the pheasants' enclosure.

which Saxony fought on the side of Napoleon, the victorious allies appointed him governor-general of Saxony. He founded a new authority headed by Ernst Georg Heinrich von Carlowitz, governor and chamberlain. The Großer Garten, which had suffered severe devastation during the battle for Dresden, was opened to the public. The surrounding walls were demolished and pheasant-breeding was discontinued. From that time on, all Dresdeners without exception were able to enjoy themselves under the trees.

The palace is the Großer Garten's centrepoint. Nowhere else in the city has Louis XIV's idea of the absolute ruler as the centre of power, as expressed in the dictum »L'état c'est moi,« been better illustrated in a work of architecture. The main avenue and those at right angles to it all lead to the palace. Inside, in the middle of the building, is the great banqueting hall, from which one can look out in all four directions. That is what makes the palace in the Großer Garten, whose interior was badly damaged by fire-bombs, so valuable in terms of cultural history. Repair and restoration works have been under way for some time.

Walking from the town along the main avenue toward the palace. The sandstone, the shells and climbing plants have become blackened. Two double flights of steps hug the contours of the building. The facades are very ornate. Nine windows divide the front elevation. Larger-than-life sandstone figures stand in the niches, busts and medallions adorn the front. A central risalto lends the summer-palace calm and composure. Ornamental vases sit astride the ridge of the new roof. A host of shapes, full-length figures and masks are immortalised in the building's sandstone walls, in a paean to themes and figures of antiquity.

The palace in the Großer Garten was the first Baroque building in the Electorate of Saxony. It acted as a torch light-

The park railway

ing the way for all the rest. The Baroque way of building, though it did not make a complete break with the Renaissance, had conquered space and effect. The foundation had been laid for a new understanding of style in Dresden. Subsequent builders were unable to ignore the summer palace. The Taschenbergpalais by the Schloss, the Zwinger, and the town palace inside the fortress walls would have been inconceivable without it.

The Großer Garten palace was designed by Johann Georg Starcke, a German architect and master builder. Architectural and art historians have racked their brains to find earlier examples of this style of building. The influence of French chateau architecture is unmistakable, say some, while others claim to see an Italian sense of style. No doubt both can be discovered. Certainly, it was not built without the aid of foreign craftsmen, primarily plasterers and sculptors. No-one in Dresden at that time had mastered the new, diverse forms of

1760 and 1813 Many of the garden's original 1,500 sculptures are carried off or destroyed during fighting, and 670 lime and chestnut trees in the main and transverse avenue are felled.

1814 Governor-General Prince Repnin-Volkonsky approves the opening of the Großer Garten to the public. Parts of the Großer Garten are redesigned in the Romantic style.

1861 A piece of the Großer Garten is separated off for the Zoological Garden. Together with a piece of the »outer common«, the zoo is laid out according to plans by Peter Joseph Lenné.

View of one of the Courtiers' Houses

From 1873 Further redesign of the Großer Garten, retaining the basic Baroque outline, under the supervision of Johann Carl Friedrich Bouché.

From 1878 The Carola Lake and surroundings are laid out.

1887 First international horticultural show.

1890 The Großer Garten is again expanded, with the addition of the Grunau park designed by Bouché.

1893 The Botanical Garden is opened.

1926 The mosaic fountain designed by Hans Poelzig (restored in 1993) is built to mark the jubilee horticultural show.

nascent Baroque. Whatever the influences, in any case the palace is a major architectural achievement in its own right.

It was built in a period of relaxation. The Thirty Years War had ended in 1648. Saxony had recovered relatively quickly from its consequences and had begun to think about building again. Work on the palace was started in 1678 in the rule of Elector Johann Georg II. »But,« wrote Dresden art historian Fritz Löffler, »the palace and garden do not originate with him, but with the then Electoral Prince, later Elector Johann Georg III.« The palace exterior is thought to have been completed in 1683, but the interior works dragged on for a few years longer. The palace experienced some great days, the greatest of which must have been the festivities marking the marriage of Friedrich August II, then still Electoral Prince, to Archduchess Maria Josepha of the Habsburg imperial dynasty. Strangely enough, after the Augustan period and even later, the court showed little interest in the palace. In 1828 a landscape gardening business started using the corner rooms and ground floor. Parts of the palace became a kind of store. For a while the banqueting hall was used to house works by the sculptor Ernst Rietschel. Finally, the Altertumsverein, or Antiquity Association, established a museum in the summer palace. Its collections of sculptures, altars, gravestones and pictures remained in the building until they and the large Baroque ceiling frescos went up in flames in February 1945.

The coming years must show how the palace can be used. One thing seems certain, however: this early example of Baroque architecture in Germany is set to receive more attention in future than in the past few decades. In one way, however, continuity has been nicely maintained. The Großer Garten was a place of amusement for the court and the nobility, and for Dresdeners it is a wonderful piece of nature in the midst of a busy city, a garden for recreation and enjoyable walks. Happy the people who own it.

13/14 February 1945 The palace and gardens are destroyed by bombs. The palace, till then a museum and store for the Saxon Antiquity Association, is gutted.

1949–1951 First reconstruction works.

1950 The children's railway, later the Pioneers' Railway and from 1990 the Park Railway, is inaugurated. It has 5.6 kilometres of track and four stations.

1953–1957 The 5,700-seat Junge Garde Open-air Theatre, the 450-seat Sonnenhäusl Puppet Theatre and the 500-seat Park Theatre are built.

1954 Start of works to secure and rebuild the palace.

Until 1982 Reconstruction works (laying out the central flower bed and the herbaceous borders).

1993 The property is taken over by the Free State of Saxony. The 160-hectare Großer Garten becomes part of the newly established Dresden state castles and gardens administration.

1993–1995 Restoration of the sculptures »Time Abducts Beauty« by Pietro Balestra and »Time Reveals Truth« by Antonio Corradini.

A writer's wishful thinking

With words, it is not even possible to describe a chair accurately enough for master carpenter Kunze to make a replica of it in his workshop! So much the less Schloss Moritzburg with its four round towers reflected in the water, or the Italian Corradini's vase by the palace lake, diagonally opposite Café Pollender. Or the Zwinger's Crown Gate. I see already that I shall have to ask the illustrator to make a series of drawings for this chapter. So that you, on seeing them, can get at least some idea and feeling of how lovely my home town was!

Perhaps I will even ask him whether he has time to draw one of the Courtiers' Houses that flank the palace in the Großer Garten. As a young man, I thought: »You'd like to live in one of those for the rest of your life. Maybe you'll be famous one day, and then the mayor will come along, wearing his golden neck-chain, and present it to you on behalf of city.« I would have moved in with my library. In the mornings, I would have breakfasted in the palace café and fed the swans. After that I would have taken a walk through the old avenues, the grove of blooming rhododendrons, and right round the Carola lake. At mid-day the courtier would have made himself two fried eggs and then, with the window open, treated himself to a nap. Later, I would have gone just round the corner to the zoo. Or to the Great Flower Exhibition. Or to the Hygiene Museum. Or to the horse-races in Reick. And at night, again with the window open, I would have slept marvellously. I would have dreamed about Augustus the Strong, about Aurora von Königsmarck and about the beautiful, hapless Countess Cosel.

You want to know when I would have worked? How can one be so nosy? The brownies would have taken care of that, the descendants of the royal Polish and Saxon court dwarves! Very small, very capable people. After brief instructions from me, they would have written my poems and novels on miniature typewriters, while I galloped along the wide, dark-brown bridle ways on dapple-grey Almansor, my favourite horse. As far as the Picardy, where I and Almansor would have drunk coffee and eaten streusel cake!

Kästner, E.: Als ich ein kleiner Junge war

Regal Pillnitz

Approach it time and again, and ever-new is the feeling that Pillnitz, charming Pillnitz, has an air of the South. And the certainty remains that when the dear Lord created this landscape he must have been in the best of his creator's moods. The tree-rich gentle hills on which magnificent vines flourish. The New Palace, the plain chapel wing. Dully gleaming slate and classy grey tones on facades of the classical simplicity which followed Baroque. A passage leads to the Lilac Courtyard, which is open on one side. When the lilac blossoms in spring, when the magnificent show of flowers in the pleasure-garden bursts into bloom, when the River Elbe laps quietly against the great flight of steps, one should by all means close ones eyes. The people who built by this river did so with great confidence.

The wooden gate to the palace garden stands open. On the right, facing the hills, is the hillside palace, on the left the waterside palace. These are the oldest parts of Schloss Pillnitz. In the shadows of the park, surprises lie in wait: the orangerie, whose central section dates back to the Augustan era, the English and Chinese pavilions and the tall old Japanese camellia in its new steel and glass house. More than 250 years old, it is a rarity in European gardens. From the pleasure-garden, the view is straight ahead to the hedge areas, to the chestnut-lined Mailbahn, leading into the open countryside. Out of the garden into the wide open spaces. Just as those who drew up the plans for Schloss Pillnitz intended.

The two palaces, the hillside palace and the waterside palace, are among the leading attractions of German architecture. It was probably the first time in Germany, indeed in Europe, that an »Indian-style« palace was built outside the gates of the Elector's royal capital. Admiration for Far Eastern

Page 35:
The hillside palace

The English Pavilion

1206 Documentary evidence exists of a manor in Pillnitz, in the burgraviate of Dohna.

1335 First mention of the village of Pillnitz.

After 1403 The old palace is mentioned under various owners.

1609 Pleasure garden and summerhouse are built.

1616 The palace is extended into a four-winged building.

1694 Johann Georg IV buys Pillnitz manor for his mistress Magdalena Sibylle von Neitschütz. After their deaths, the manor passes to the new Elector, Friedrich August I.

1706–1718 Countess Cosel owns Pillnitz, a gift from the Elector.

1718 The palace returns to Augustus the Strong. He now implements his plans in the context of a large-scale palace-building programme inspired by French palace architecture.

1720–1730 The complex is redesigned under August the Strong. The waterside and hillside palaces are built to designs by Matthäus Daniel Pöppelmann. The 1596 church is demolished. The ring-racing building, the Temple of Venus, the Vineyard Church, the pleasure garden and the great palace garden are all constructed.

1768–1918 Summer residence of the Saxon court.

objects, for »oriental ways,« was a keynote of the feeling for life at Baroque courts. Travellers' reports had drawn people's attention to far-off lands. They described a life in cheerful surroundings and told of fabulous wealth at the foreign courts. Encounters and confrontations with the Turks, who marched to the outskirts of Vienna for the last time in 1683, had also promoted an interest in foreign cultures. Chinese and Japanese porcelain were regarded as particular treasures. China worship had come into fashion at German courts. Augustus the Strong, who commissioned Schloss Pillnitz, was also an admirer of things oriental, of the exotic world. He wanted his own »Indian palace« in Pillnitz. Matthäus Daniel Pöppelmann, the king's architect, and others built it for him. It was they who put the curved roofs on the palaces, the ridge turrets and dragons and weather-vanes. In the hollow mouldings, artists depicted the colourful world of oriental folk life, dream worlds they had never seen.

Originally, Pillnitz was a modest manor. Soon, it was joined by a church. A Renaissance castle adorned the village. Vines and fruit trees flourished. As early as 1403, a document mentions the »Pillnitz wine hills.« Elector Augustus tried to gain possession of the estate in 1578. He failed. After that, it changed hands several times. Not until Johann Georg IV, the brother of Augustus the Strong, did the ruler succeed. He bought the castle and estate from the Bünau family and transferred ownership to his mistress, Magdalena Sibylle von Neitschütz. Her good fortune was short-lived. They both died of smallpox in 1694. After that, Pillnitz reverted to the House of Wettin. Soon, it was to belong to another mistress, Countess Cosel. She was given it in the heyday of their passion, when she had been elevated to the status of Augustus's official mistress. They are said to have often stayed in Pillnitz. Even in those days, there was a flight of steps leading from the Elbe to

View of the hillside palace

the old Renaissance castle. They must surely have enjoyed the countryside, the hillside vineyards, riding through the forest. Countess Cosel often stayed in Pillnitz, which brought her a lot of money. She extended the clipped Charmillen, as the hornbeam hedges were called, where courtly society devoted itself to its games and seductions. When she fell into disfavour and was banished to Stolpen, Augustus the Strong reclaimed Pillnitz. It remains a mystery why he ordered the wedding of Auguste Constantine, his erstwhile mistress's oldest daughter, to be celebrated at Schloss Pillnitz of all places. Friedrich August III elevated Pillnitz, which had previously been used mostly as a place for summer amusement, to his main summer residence.

Major construction works started in 1720 with the building of the fine staircase guarded by two sphinxes. Instead of the old Renaissance castle, which burned down in 1818, Christian Friedrich Schuricht built the New Palace for King

1778–1791 A new building phase starts with the extension of the palace park in the English style, probably according to plans by Johann Daniel Schade (c. 2780), building of the palace wings designed by Christian Traugott Weinlig, and the Dutch and Chinese gardens (pavilion by Christian Friedrich Schuricht, 1804). Japanese camellia arrives in Pillnitz c.1770.

1791 The Pillnitz Declaration.

1818 The old palace is destroyed by fire.

1818–1826 Third building phase. Building of Schuricht's New Palace with kitchen and chapel wing. An imposing domed hall (Dresden's only classical-style dome), with interior paintings by court painter Carl Christian Vogel (later Vogel von Vogelstein). Vogel also paints the interior of the Catholic palace chapel (restored 1974–1977).

1838–1867 The pleasure garden is reshaped, after 1864, to plans by Peter Joseph Lenné.

1858–1861 Building of the palm house.

After 1866 The lilac courtyard is planted.

1874–1880 The play garden is redesigned and the orangerie extended.

1924 Pillnitz passes into public ownership and serves as dwellings, studios and other artists' workshops.

1942–1945 Schloss Pillnitz houses works of art removed from Dresden.

2 March 1945 During the seventh air-raid on Dresden, the stable building, the orangerie, the palm house and the court gardener's house are damaged or destroyed, but not the palace.

1946 The Central Museum in the State of Saxony is opened in the palace with the remaining works from the Dresden art gallery.

1952–1993 Pillnitz palace and park are managed by the municipality of Dresden.

1963 The Arts and Crafts Museum is opened in the waterside palace.

1993 Pillnitz palace and park become part of the Dresden state castles and gardens administration.

The Vineyard Church

Friedrich August I. We have Schuricht and others to thank for the fact that the palace and grounds still feel like an integrated whole. Though a classicist architect himself, he adapted to Pöppelmann and Longuelune, recreating their Baroque feeling for form, though with more restrained and less lavish »Chinese« details, but with great respect for what already existed and for his predecessors' architectural achievement. So a piece of architecture from the first third of the 18th century was left undisturbed and the melody of nature and stone was unimpaired.

A slight wind stirs in the conifer grove. A rustle goes through the old trees in the park. Several generations influenced it, electors, kings, botanists and gardeners. The sphinxes look at the river flowing at a leisurely pace toward downtown Dresden. It is time to go inside the palace. One is richly rewarded with craftwork, with old furniture, musical instruments and glasses, with Dutch and French faïence.

King Johann the poet

»Philalethes,« the scholarly translator of Dante, whom Friedrich Wilhelm IV always called »my brother-in-law the professor,« also proved himself an imaginative and skilful writer of occasional poems, as the following verses show:

On the fire at Schloss Pillnitz, 1 May 1818

Oh tranquil scene of my youthful pleasure
Where I savoured childhood's golden dream
Where life passed by me without a care
Now I am to part from your sight

That oft poured balm into my sore heart
My eye is never again to feast
On the friendly buildings of your temple
On your familiar old palace.

The column of smoke climbs up to heaven
Oh, thus vanishes every earthly happiness
And returns to the nothing from which it came.

Even our life's course escapes in haste.
So let us turn our gaze heavenward
That one day every wound may heal up there.

From: Haenel, E.; Kalkschmidt, E. (Eds.):
Das alte Dresden. Frankfurt am Main, 1977, p. 217

Barockschloss Rammenau

Rammenau – a blend of ochre and green

The Barockschloss Rammenau (Baroque palace of Rammenau) is idyllic. A poet would sing its praises in iambic pentameters. Swallows' nests cling beneath the arched gateway. A pair of storks has built its nest on the roof of the eastern Courtiers' House. All the while they keep coming back and breeding young, the pond landscape around the place is intact. Anyone coming from Bischofswerda, the gateway to the Oberlausitz region, will be anointed with shades of green and the pond surfaces will flash. The countryside rests in summer ripeness, in expectation of autumn. From the gatehouse a cobbled way leads up to the palace, lined with linden trees and interrupted by a flower-filled circular bed. In its middle stands a magnificent vase, and sandstone figures surround the circle. Two side wings frame the front of the building, which is slightly set back. A flight of stone steps leads to the entrance portal.

The Baroque palace testifies to the Saxon nobility's refined sense of architecture. The town palaces and castles built in the royal capital Dresden and its surroundings in the Augustan period (1694–1763) were soon creatively imitated by the landed aristocracy. Manor houses and palaces were one way in which the Saxon nobility, which successfully resisted Augustus the Strong's attempts to be an absolute ruler, demonstrated its own ambitions. Rammenau is an example. No unimportant architect can have built this distinguished country palace, for it was executed with great mastery. Although there is nothing in writing to prove it, architectural historians ascribe the Baroque Palace of Rammenau to the Dresden head state architect Johann Christoph Knöffel. He was a pupil of Daniel Pöppelmann's and Count Brühl's favourite architect. The country palace was built for Ernst Ferdinand von Knoch, chamberlain to the Elector of Saxony and King of Poland,

Page 43: Staircase

View of the castle and main courtyard

1241 First documentary mention of Rammenau in the Oberlausitz border charter.

1717 Ernst Ferdinand von Knoch, chamberlain to the King of Poland and Elector of Saxony, buys the manor.

From 1721 the Baroque palace is built under the supervision of Erst Ferdinand von Knoch, possibly according to designs by the Saxon architect Johann Christoph Knöffel. The building overstretches its client's financial resources, and so in

1744 it passes to Franz Joseph von Hoffmann, councillor and privy chamberlain to the King of Poland and Elector of Saxony.

1750 Johann Albericus von Hoffmann, secretary of the Electorate of Saxony legation in London, inherits the whole estate, is elevated to the status of Imperial Count in 1778 and bears the title von Hoffmannsegg.

1762 The philosopher Johann Gottlieb Fichte is born in Rammenau.

1788 Johann Centurius von Hoffmannsegg inherits Rammenau from his father. He is one of the leading naturalists of his day.

1794 Friedrich von Kleist, cavalry captain and Knight of the Order of St. John, buys the castle. He is one of the leading builders in the palace's architectural history. He has the palace and grounds redesigned in the classicist style in which they can largely be seen today.

Canvas wall-covering in the Chinese Room

who had bought Rammenau manor for 36,000 talers. Evidently Knoch had overstretched himself financially, because soon afterwards he had to sell the property. In the centuries that followed, it often changed hands, but that seems not to have done the palace any harm, as the continuation of building works shows. The Baroque palace passed into state ownership in 1945. Conservationists took an interest in it and in the 1960s and 1970s restored it to a good condition. Students from the Dresden College of Art cared for it. Now, it is one of the best preserved palaces in Saxony.

The harmony outside that makes one curious to see the palace continues in the building's interior. The entrance hall is imposing, the Baroque staircase beautiful, the Hall of Mirrors luxurious. Trompe l'oeil paintings make the spaces look bigger. Shades of pink, green and ochre, gold and red paint delicate pictures full of atmosphere. Every room, every salon, has its unmistakable design. Magnificent crystal chandeliers send out a shower of warm light. The Baroque palace has something that is no longer found very often in Saxony. In the Chinese Room, the fashion for chinoiserie that inspired artists and rulers in the period of absolutism, is paid homage to in a blaze of colours. Imaginary scenes from Chinese life dating back to Knoch's day are painted on canvas wall-coverings. Picture sequences show a light-hearted everyday life, with people riding on elephants, drinking, singing, playing the flute, aiming at exotic birds. Connoisseurs think the wall-coverings were painted in around 1735. The Baroque palace of Rammenau has its own very special magic. Hardly a palace in Saxony is so vibrant with light-hearted cheer, almost as if a leading composer had produced a marvellous score. The lords of the palace, at any rate, recognised this long ago. Schloss Rammenau concerts held in the Hall of Mirrors in front of the Baroque fireplace and under the great chandelier have been drawing music-lovers for many years.

Rammenau is the birthplace of philosopher Johann Gottlieb Fichte, 1762–1814, who in his »Reden an die deutsche Nation« (Speeches to the German Nation) spoke out passionately against despotic princes and foreign domination by Napoleon. Local people have devoted attention to his works and influence for a long time. He is remembered in a small museum in the palace, which was redesigned after German reunification. It is indeed a place worthy of a man who came from very poor circumstances and was able to gain an education because a nobleman, von Militz, recognised young Fichte's talent and enabled him to go to school. Thus the wheel turns full circle. The palace, built, reshaped and cared

1820 Johann Centurius von Hoffmannsegg buys back the estate because he wants to spend his declining years in Schloss Rammenau. His son Conradin von Hoffmannsegg sells it in 1880 to Hans Curt Christoph Ernst von Posern, chamberlain to the King of Saxony and monastery steward of Marienstern.

1884 The estate passes by way of inheritance to the von Helldorff family (until 1945).

1942 Parts of the Dresden art collections are stored at the palace for safe-keeping.

1945 The land reform expropriates the owners. Schloss Rammenau is externally well preserved and has not suffered from the war. However, parts of the interior are damaged.

1948 The property passes to the state of Saxony's Ministry of Education.

1951 The palace is used by the Dresden College of Fine Arts.

1954 Initial restoration works begin.

1962 The town's Fichte memorial is moved to the palace. Extensive restoration works are begun.

1963 Bischofswerda county council takes over responsibility for the palace.

1966 The county museum is opened.

1970 The Dresden Cultural Academy starts using the palace (for lectures and as a boarding school).

1974 By now, 1.5 million visitors have visited the palace and gardens.

1993 Barockschloss Rammenau passes into the ownership of the Free State of Saxony and has since been managed as a state-owned castle enterprise.

1995 The restored Hall of Mirrors is reopened.

for by architecturally-minded people, is now elevated by a man who certainly had no access to it in those days.

Back into the open air, into the shimmering light of the English-style park adjoining the palace. Here, too, it was the nearby royal seat of the Wettin rulers that showed the way. When the Großer Garten in Dresden was extended and rede-

»The Devil's Room«

View of the palace from the park

signed in the romantic style, the owners of Schloss Rammenau, not to be outdone, commissioned their own English landscaped garden. Indeed, the educated, art-minded Saxon nobility in the countryside could definitely keep up with the men who commissioned buildings in the sparkling capital. Luckily for the country and a challenge to the Free State to maintain the glory of a heritage so perfectly designed.

Two young storks stretch their necks and clatter their beaks. A concert is scheduled to take place in the park this August Sunday. Perhaps it doesn't need to be iambic pentameters after all, the rise and fall of syllables, that sings the park's and the palace's praises. As flute and cello sound in the Hall of Mirrors and the palace restaurant hospitably receives diners, the visitor is absorbed in a blend of ochre and green. And that alone is enough of the great many pleasures that Rammenau can give.

The Devil's Room

When Ernst Ferdinand von Knoch, a chamberlain of the Elector of Saxony, bought the manor in 1717, he immediately set about rearranging the manor and palace buildings. He had the Kleppischteiche ponds laid dry, some places filled in and the present buildings constructed on the site. The building works carried on from 1721 to 1737 and cost enormous sums of money that soon undermined the chamberlain's financial circumstances, so much so, that in 1744 he had to flee from his creditors. One day, when no real progress was being made with building the palace in Rammenau because the money the chamberlain had available was insufficient, the devil appeared to him. The devil likes to seek out poor people or misers who have fallen into difficulties, so as to capture their souls. He offered to help with finishing the palace. Soon the two parties came to an agreement, and the palace grew to completion. Gradually, it became clearer and clearer that the devil had demanded something in return for his willingness to help, for there was one room in the palace that nobody was allowed to enter. It was always kept firmly closed. But even the strongly-bolted door could not prevent a constant stench of pitch and sulphur from leaking out.

From that time on people knew that the chamberlain had been forced to concede one room to the devil. It is known as the devil's room to this day.

The devil likes to avoid being seen by the general public. Here, too, he wanted to enter and leave unseen. So he had asked for a separate entrance and exit, which he made himself in a single night, disguising it as a chimney. But even he could not prevent the chamberlain's subsequent flight from his creditors, and soon it was said that the devil had taken him.

Note

The palace really does have a devil's room, and it is still closed to visitors, as it is used for internal purposes. The name stems from the wall-painting motifs in this room, in which a blind chimney was installed for the sake of symmetry.

Author unknown

Burg Stolpen

Life imprisonment in Burg Stolpen

It exudes an air of mystery. Perhaps it's because of the colour of the stone, which displays many shades in the changing light. Built on a high basalt cliff, Burg Stolpen (Stolpen Castle) was fought over, occupied and hated. The bishops of Meißen who owned the castle for a long time, resided in Stolpen. Once, when their funds ran low, they pawned it. Under the castle's protection they resisted the Reformation's introduction in Albertinian Saxony. Their efforts and prayers were in vain. The progress of the former Augustinian monk Martin Luther's doctrine was inexorable. Elector Augustus forced the bishop to give him the castle, the town and his lordship over the area in an advantageous swap. Hussites besieged the castle's steep walls and withdrew without success. Croatian, Swedish, Habsburg and Prussian troops were deployed in front of it and devastated it. Prussian Hussars occupied it. Napoleon ordered the castle to be taken and met with no resistance. When he withdrew, his troops blew up part of the buildings. But that was to be of no help to him.

The castle fell into serious decay. Nonetheless, enough has survived of this fortress founded in the then Slavic Milzen area, with its towers and gates, battlements and courtyards, fountains and vaults, torture chamber and oubliette. All of this can be seen at the castle. Above all, however, Stolpen has become famous as epitomising the arbitrariness of a ruler. Countess Cosel, Friedrich August's best-known mistress, was banished to the basalt cliff and spent 49 years in captivity at Stolpen. Those who write or claim that Countess Cosel was reluctant to part company with Stolpen are wrong. That legend has been woven to make her end seem harmonious.

Page 51: The Johannisturm, or Cosel Tower

The sorry condition of the castle and outbuildings must have grieved local history enthusiasts, but also other far-

The Seigerturm and Seven-Pointed Tower seen from the Johannisturm

A bird's-eye view of castle and town

1222 First verified mention of a manor of the nobleman Moyko von Stolpen, administrative centre and secondary residence of the Bishops of Meißen.

1347 Assistance treaty between the Bishop and the Burgrave of Meißen. The Bishop awards the Stolpen fortress to the Burgrave.

Since 1365 The castle is temporarily a clerical court and a prison of the Meißen episcopate.

1429 Hussites lay siege to the castle for nearly eight weeks without success.

sighted people. Gradually, they became active in recalling the castle's history. A society began collecting antiquities. In 1874, a great moment for both the castle and town arrived. The castle, in which the first modest collections had been housed, was opened to the public. It developed into a museum. When King Friedrich August III of Saxony visited Burg Stolpen in 1904 and ordered its renovation, the former bishop's residence caught the public eye. That has remained so to the present day.

Countess Cosel's fate is portrayed in the Johannisturm tower. It was Christmas 1716 when an escort brought her from Nossen to Stolpen. It is not known whether the countryside was covered in snow. Did she even think about it being Christmas? She didn't feel well, she was ill. She had left chilly Nossen on the Freiberg Mulde behind her. Soon after her arrival, by order of Augustus the Strong, the guard was reinforced by 40 soldiers and four corporals. The Elector forbade the prisoner to have any contact with the outside world. He wrote in his own hand: »Nobody is to be allowed into the castle without the prior knowledge of the Major and of Captain Heinicken, and the Major will inform the latter of everything and not allow anything to happen without his prior knowledge. The windows in the room of the detained person must be kept safe so that she cannot hold a conversation through them with anyone, except with those who are expressly allowed to do so; but especially the said detainee must be prevented from speaking with the sentries and especially industrious attention must be paid to this...« He goes on to say: »If the Countess wants to go for a walk in the zoo garden at any time, she is to be permitted to do so, however the Major and the Captain are to accompany her, but first some sentries must be posted around the zoo garden, and the avenues and concealed places must be properly inspected beforehand...«

Imagine what Countess Cosel must have been thinking in the inhospitality of the castle high on the basalt hilltop. What had she done to the Elector, who had sworn eternal fidelity to her, to make him punish her so severely? He had promised to marry her if his wife were to die, and she had borne him three children. She will have found no answer. And there is no answer as to why she was banished for life. Was it hatred? Had it not wounded the Elector that she rebelled against him, that she did not return his promise of marriage? She did not accept her imprisonment passively. Time and again, she begged the Elector to restore her liberty. He remained unmoved, asking

From 1451 The castle complex is greatly extended. Especially noteworthy: the material used is almost exclusively local basalt, which has helped the castle to maintain its unique, durable appearance until the present day.

1520 Bishop Johann VII of Schleinitz issues the Stolpen Decree (first official order against Martin Luther). The bishops resist the Reformation's introduction in the Stolpen region until 1558. The castle is their chief residence.

1539 The most precious relics of the episcopate of Meißen are stored in Stolpen Castle.

18 January 1559 Elector Augustus of Saxony takes over the castle, town and lordship of Stolpen in an exchange.

From 1559 The fortress is altered and expanded. A zoological garden is laid out on the southern slope below the castle, which develops into an imposing residence and official headquarters for the Elector and his family.

1563 A hydraulic system designed by the Freiberg architect Martin Planer is installed.

1618–1648 Castle and town suffer serious destruction during the Thirty Years War.

1634 A permanent garrison is established at the castle.

1675 Wolf Caspar von Klengel's buildings give Stolpen the features of a modern fortress.

1716 Countess Cosel, mistress of Augustus the Strong, starts her 49-year imprisonment.

1723 A devastating fire destroys Stolpen town centre and parts of the castle.

1756 The Prussians occupy the castle. Extensive destruction is wrought during their retreat.

1764 The garrison is disbanded and Stolpen deleted from the list of Saxon fortresses. The castle and outbuildings fall victim to natural decay.

1773 Head state architect Exner orders dilapidated parts of the castle to be demolished.

1813 Napoleon has defence buildings constructed. Stolpen is spared fighting, but large sections of the castle are blown up by retreating French troops at the end of September.

1842 A park is laid out on the upper southern slope below the castle.

1859 King Johann of Saxony orders extensive works to secure and renovate the buildings.

1874 A castle custodian is appointed. A collection of antiquities assembled by Stolpen societies provides the foundation for the museum.

1883 The castle well, filled in in 1756 and 1813, is cleared on the initiative of the Königlich-Sächsisches Altertumsverein (Royal Saxon Antiquity Society).

»But how can one rely on you when you have broken your word so often?« He did not say which word, and there is no way of knowing what he really had to reproach her for. The authorities suggested he should justify imprisoning her because of »her malice, her meanness, her intrigues and her bad conduct.« That was too little, even for the Elector. Augustus the Strong died in February 1733. By then, Countess Cosel had been a prisoner for nearly 17 years. In a letter dated 8 March 1733 she wrote: »It is extremely cold up here, and there is much snow and wind, due to which rheumatic throats and other ailments have also affected my servants. With me, things are always the same – one day passes like another. So I pine away until the good Lord...« It is certain that she hoped

The castle at night

to be released after his death. She hoped in vain. Friedrich August II did not release her either. He and the Dresden court were indifferent to her fate. Another 32 years were to pass after Augustus the Strong's death before she died in March 1765. Her fate is moving still today, nearly 250 years later. In the Johannisturm, she comes to life in paintings. She lay on this bed (it is no longer the bed she actually slept in), she warmed herself in front of this stove, she drank from this glass, she read these books, she embroidered this coat-of-arms. And anyone looking out of the tower windows sees what she saw, the town of Stolpen, the villages, the Lausitz hill country, the sweeping Elbe sandstone mountains.

Undoubtedly, it is this woman's fate that attracts tens of thousands of visitors each year. But Burg Stolpen has more to offer, including a unique hydraulic system (replica) which supplied the town and castle with water, the gloomy torture chamber, an amazing basalt fountain, an exciting example of what nature and time shaped and formed – the Stolpen basalt rock, which is reminiscent of organ-pipes and honeycombs. From this basalt the castle was built, on this basalt hilltop stand the towers and walls. It was the hardness of the stone which enabled the castle to survive even after it was maltreated, plundered and razed. And the care of those far-sighted people.

1904 King Friedrich August III of Saxony visits the castle. A sum of 4,000 to 5,000 Marks per year is to be used to maintain the castle.

1933–1938 Extensive works to secure the building are undertaken.

1946 The castle is taken into management by the Dresden state museums, castles and gardens administration.

1957 The town of Stolpen assumes legal responsibility for the castle.

From 1960 The castle is used as a backdrop for numerous film shoots and used intensively for cultural purposes.

1973 Extensive works begin to maintain the quality of the Johannisturm (Cosel tower).

Since 1993 Stolpen has been a state-owned castle enterprise.

1994 The newly designed Countess Cosel exhibition is opened.

The treasure by the town wall

A town filled so often with the events of war that was forced to suffer fire and hunger and bloodshed and disease is bound to have a host of buried treasures. The old people have many tales to tell about them, but so far all that has been found is the occasional old coin or two. But one treasure is definitely buried by the old town wall, in a spot between two houses (Wiegand and Schmidt). Anyone who is not one of those newfangled know-it-alls sees, between midnight and one o'clock in the morning a motionless white flame in the garden. But he must have been born on a Sunday and baptised on Palm Sunday, otherwise it won't work. As he approaches the white flame, he must say: »Oh flame, white and soft, come, I want to save you and you are to give me your treasures!« Then, he must embrace the white flame. The flame turns into a white lily. At its roots lies the treasure, and when he has dug out the roots he will find a white virgin there. He must marry her, and in return he will receive a boundless treasure. Nobody knows how the enchanted virgin got there and why she has to guard the treasure. Some say she was a rich young townswoman who planned to buy her beloved's freedom with her gold after he was taken prisoner by the Croats, but who met with an accident while jumping over the wall. Others believe she is Countess Cosel or a noblewoman from the days when only a castle stood here, and no town.

People born as the midday bells are ringing on Palm Sunday have also seen a white figure holding a candle in its hand walking round the flame. That would indicate that it is more likely to be Countess Cosel looking for her treasures that she had kept in safe hiding-places.

Schmolke, H.: Der Schatz an der Stadtmauer. In: Mitteldeutsche Blätter für Volkskunde, Leipzig, 1934. No. 2, p. 65.

KASSE

A fortress without gloom

Festung Königstein (Königstein Fortress) is in the region known as Saxon Switzerland. The mighty defensive complex is built on a rock. The buildings, which stand on a plateau on top, resemble a small garrison and fortress town. It had everything necessary to survive and defend itself over a prolonged period – a well and a church, a military hospital and barracks, an armoury and a wine-cellar, a schoolroom and stables. In times of peace the soldiers practised crafts. There was plenty of building to do, in those days as now.

The history of the fortress that started out as a castle goes back a long way. Nothing remains of the caste except a few relics in the garrison church and in the Georgenburg (George's Castle). But the later buildings on the flat-topped hill are well worth seeing. Buildings and crenels, gateways and casemates turn out to be major works of architecture.

Situated in the border country between Bohemia and the March of Meißen, Königstein was courted and fought over by both. Anyone who occupied it and paid enough men to fight had the Elbe Valley and the river under his control. Finally, the Wettins prevailed and Königstein was lost to the rulers of Bohemia. A spate of building activity began under Elector Christian I, 1586–1591, who ordered »the castle to be built completely into a proper fortress.« From then on, Königstein was closely linked with Saxon history.

It was a border fort and a place of refuge, a place for court outings, a treasure-house, a state prison and used to house prisoners of war. Above all, however, the fortress was feared, and rightly so. People who fell out of favour at court in Dresden and were detained in Königstein could usually bid their lives farewell. Escape was virtually ruled out. The walls were too steep, the rock too high, the security too tight.

Page 59:
The fortress entrance and Georgenburg

The fortress towers high above the River Elbe

Nikolaus Krell, chancellor of the Electorate of Saxony, who had made enemies of both the aristocracy and the Lutheran clergy, spent ten years imprisoned in Königstein before being executed in Dresden. Occasionally, important personages were brought to Königstein for security reasons. Johann Friedrich Böttger, the inventor of European porcelain, is said to have foamed with rage when he was taken to Königstein in summer 1706 and assigned to quarters in the Georgenburg. Nobody was to know Böttger's whereabouts. He was described as a »gentleman with three servants.« But Böttger was no meek and mild inmate. He demanded French wine and

The castle

1241 King Wenceslas I of Bohemia signs the Oberlausitz border treaty »in lapide regis« (»on the king's stone, or in German the »Königstein«), the first mention of a castle on the Königstein.

1359 Emperor Charles IV signs several documents in the »imperial castle« (the Georgenburg).

1406/08 The castle is twice besieged and captured by the Margrave of Meißen.

1428/43 The brewery and the hill house (later the Magdalenenburg and the commandant's house) are built.

1459 The treaty of Eger provides for Königstein to be permanently integrated in the March of Meißen under Bohemian sovereignty.

1516–1526 A Celestine monastery is established, but dissolved again.

1563–1569 Master mining engineer Martin Planer of Freiberg supervises the sinking of the well (152.47 metres deep).

1576 The Elector receives a report that »now the Königstein (stands) very deserted and desolate.«

The fortress

1589 Elector Christian I orders the former castle to be »completely turned into a proper fortress.« The foundation stone is laid for the Christiansburg (later the Friedrichsburg). The south entrance is closed. A new way up is created on the west side, and work is started on the gatehouse, the ramparts and the barracks.

Since 1591 State prison. Among those imprisoned here were Chancellor Nikolaus Krell (1591), Johann Friedrich Böttger (1706/07), Michail Bakunin (1849/50), and August Bebel.

1594 The Old Armoury is completed.

1619 The Georgenburg is formally opened.

game. This unsettled the fortress commandant, and that will have pleased Böttger. Still, he did not receive any more wine than his ration. The prisoner is said to have smashed »the glass against the wall« in rage. Böttger, who had promised to make gold, was not to fall into the hands of the Swedes who had occupied Saxony in the Northern War. In the Georgenburg, part of his life is reproduced. Later, the fortress housed »traitors to the fatherland« such as the revolutionary and anarchist Mikhail Bakunin, who had taken part in the May 1849 Dresden uprising, the socialist August Bebel and the caustic Expressionist writer Frank Wedekind.

In wartime the Saxon court fled to the fortress because it was considered to be impregnable. When the Saxon army capitulated to the Prussians in 1756, Elector Friedrich August II hurried to the protection of its walls, along with his cour-

Inside the commandant's rooms

tiers and leading ministers, including Heinrich Graf von Brühl. Frederick the Great, who had forced the Saxon army to capitulate in the shadow of the Lilienstein, generously allowed the Elector to withdraw to Poland. There Friedrich August, who was also King of Poland, waited until the end of the Seven Years War, which Saxony ended losing.

The plateau, shaded by ancient trees, can be reached by elevator and on foot, walking up through three gateways to the New Armoury. The poor horses who used to have to climb up here! On top, there is usually a breeze, and across the parapet one has a view of the Elbe and Biele valleys. Some landscapes are truly breathtaking. The great bend in the Elbe, slate-coloured, the Lilienstein on the right bank in its magical autumn colours, the bizarre rock formations of Saxon Switzerland, the plains in ever-changing light, ochre-shaded paths, gracefully laid out villages and small towns.

There is hardly any of the sense of foreboding usually associated with fortresses, though Königstein did not lose its military significance until after 1900. Neither the cannons nor the crenels look threatening. The buildings communicate, they are »exhibits of themselves.« Königstein Fortress, an open-air museum of buildings, was usually well looked after. Recently, it gained a further attraction. A piece of history sparkles. In the basement of the renovated treasure-house, coins can be seen gleaming in a barrel. They are protected by trapdoors. A soldier stands guard, his nose red with exertion. (Red noses are said to have been a common phenomenon in the garrison, as the wine-cellars prove, understandably after the dreary duty in stony isolation.) A well-dressed official sits at the table making entries in a record. This tableau is a reminder that in times of threat it was not only electors and kings who fled to Königstein. The state treasures were also stored in the basement safes – gold and silver bars, jewellery and other items, inclu-

1621/22 The brewery is converted into a small Renaissance palace (the Magdalenenburg).

1631 The Johannissaal hall is built above the Dunkle Appareille.

1669–1679 The Georgenbatterie is built in front of the Georgenbau under the supervision of Wolf Caspar von Klengel.

1676–1689 The castle chapel is converted into a garrison church and a garrison cemetery is laid out.

1698 and 1712 Tsar Peter I of Russia visits Königstein.

1715 The architect Matthäus Daniel Pöppelmann builds a stone pump-room.

1722–1725 The giant wine barrel, with a capacity of 240,000 litres, is installed in the Magdalenenburg.

1729–1735 The Dunkle Appareille is deepened, new outer works are built, and the Christiansburg is altered and renamed the Friedrichsburg.

1735/36 Six small powder magazines are installed. One has been preserved.

1756 The Prussian army takes 17,000 Saxons prisoner on the Lilienstein plateau. The Königstein fortress is declared neutral territory.

1767 Building of the casemates on the southwest side of the fortress is started

1790 The lower outer works in front of the castle are built.

1806–1817 After a roof-truss fire in the gatehouse/ramparts/Johannissaal area, the Johannissaal is rebuilt as the New Armoury.

1813 Napoleon visits. The French Vandamme army corps crosses the Elbe under the fortress's protection.

1819–1822 The Magdalenenburg is converted into a bomb-proof provisions store.

1831 The fortress is placed under the authority of the war ministry. The bourgeois revolutionaries Bertholdi and Mossdorf are taken there.

1848 The 18-year-old chimney sweep Abratzky climbs the fortress wall.

1849 The Saxon royal family flees to the fortress. Some members of the bourgeois provisional government are interned.

1850 An underground telegraph link between Dresden and Königstein fortress is started up.

1854/55 A bomb-proof treasure house is built. In former times of war, too, the fortress was a place of safe-keeping for state treasure, works of art and archives.

1870/71 The fortress is used as a camp for French prisoners of war. Battery ramparts are erected for all-round defence.

1871–1899 The fortress is expanded into a fortress of the German Reich.

The Friedrichsburg

ding works of art. From 1860 to 1865, two million talers were held here for safekeeping, packed in linen bags. The gleaming coins in the barrel are made of pewter and bear the likeness of King Johann, the translator of Dante. Enthusiasts can buy the coin in the museum shop for a modest sum. The Old Armoury, where weapons were and are stored, has been freshly restored. And the exterior of the small garrison church shines again. The pump-room, which was in operation until 1967, has been renovated in recent years and is working again.

At Königstein Fortress, history becomes a sensory experience. In 1241 a border treaty between King Wenceslas I of Bohemia and the Bishop of Meißen was sealed in Königstein, and the flat-topped hill entered the annals of history. One can get lost in seven and a half centuries. That is truly a reason to wander in the fountain of time. More than half a million visitors do so every year. That has had the ticket desks humming and has been good for the fortress, which aims to make itself even more attractive.

Munition-loading system for Battery 7

1878 The garrison hospital (later the peace hospital) is built.

1880–1899 War barracks and the war hospital, the battery loading systems and the other ranks' barracks are built.

1913 The German parliament, the Reichstag, deletes the commandant's post from the military budget, thus abolishing the status of fortress in the military sense.

1914–1918 The fortress is used as a prisoner-of-war camp for Russian and French generals, officers and soldiers.

1921 A convalescent home for the Reichswehr is established.

1940–1945 The fortress is used as a prisoner-of-war camp for Polish and French generals, officers and soldiers. Parts of the Dresden art gallery and the Grünes Gewölbe collection are held there.

1949–1955 Used as a workhouse for criminal and politically troublesome juveniles.

1955 The fortress is taken over by the East German Ministry of Culture and opened as a museum.

1991 Königstein fortress is taken over by the Free State of Saxony.

From 1993 Königstein fortress is run as a state-owned castle enterprise.

Baron von Kyau

Once upon a time there lived
A Saxon-Polish general
His name was von Kyau
He was popular and well-known
At court and throughout the land
For many an amusing prank.

The king sat at his midday meal
Not far from him his general
With a very downcast look
So the king said to him
»Von Kyau, what's the matter?
You drink neither wine nor beer
Tell me, pour out your heart,
A worry shared is a worry halved.«

Kyau sighed deeply
And said, »Worry weighs heavily upon me,
I want neither beer nor wine,
I want to be king.«
The king liked a good joke
Rising straight away from his chair
He said, »Dear Kyau, I want to heal
Your pain, so for a joke
I will be von Kyau for a while
And you will be king for five minutes!«

They quickly changed places
The other diners were all listening
Wondering what would come next
But Kyau said without wavering:
»We Friedrich August by the grace of God
Do appoint von Kyau who has counselled
Us well, forthwith to be commandant
Of Königstein, with the appropriate salary
And annually 20 tuns of wine.«

King Augustus laughed heartily
And said, »That was well done,
Now go to your Königstein
And let me be king again.«

And so the new commandant
Nominated and appointed himself
Kyau was a good man
Took charge of Königstein with loving care
Jokingly called it his wife
And was both strict and meticulous in his work.

Made continuous improvements
Including building a great barrel
For keeping in Königstein
His annual 20 tuns of wine.

The barrel was the largest ever seen
It was built of oakwood
By a master's skilful hand
And tightly spanned by hoops
There must have been thirty or even more
Each weighing seven hundredweight.

No other barrel was a match for it.
In the whole Holy Roman Empire
Anyone who wants to see the rest
Let him go to the fortress!

Cf Geschichte und Sage der Festung Königstein in Sachsen, Königstein, no date, p. 28 f.

Barockgarten Großsedlitz

Barockgarten Großsedlitz – As if its maker had held his breath

For several years, a secret was kept about Barockgarten Großsedlitz (Großsedlitz Baroque Garden). Count August Christoph von Wackerbarth, an influential cabinet minister under Augustus the Strong, bought the manor of Sedlitz, complete with the villages of Großsedlitz and Kleinsedlitz. He got them cheap because a fire had destroyed the manor house in 1715. The purchase was made in 1719. The Elector's coffers were empty. His son's wedding had cost millions. Was Wackerbarth trying to prove to his master that he was a great builder too? As public works superintendent, Wackerbarth was responsible for civil and military building projects in Dresden. He was in a hurry with his plans. First, he had to remove several obstacles. The terrain was bumpy, with a large trough running through it and the ground had to be made fit for building on. As Wackerbarth was a military officer, he had soldiers work for him free of charge. The Friedrichsburg was officially opened just ten months after he had purchased the land.

Augustus the Strong must have liked what he saw being built half-way between Pirna and his capital. The palace and gardens fitted in with his plans to surround his residence with palaces and gardens. Was he envious all the same? Or was he full of praise that his cabinet minister and governor had got himself a palace and garden? Whatever the case, the Elector watched what was happening there on Dresden's doorstep very closely. And Wackerbarth gave him several opportunities to do so by inviting him to Großsedlitz. He must have told Augustus why he was building it. He wanted Großsedlitz as a place to relax. He could reach it »in two hours both by water and by land and without neglecting any official duties, relax and afterwards return to his daily duty with a much cheerier

Page 67: The view looking toward the lower orangerie

The upper orangerie

disposition. Was Wackerbarth perhaps the shrewder of the two? It had not escaped his attention that the Elector had been fired with enthusiasm.

Augustus the Strong offered to buy Großsedlitz from his minister. »Initially,« one authority said, »the count was disinclined (to sell), but his other possessions in the Radebeul Lößnitz and in Zabeltitz enabled him to do without Großsedlitz.« The purchase contract was signed in January 1723. Wackerbarth had paid 20,000 Meißen florins for Großsedlitz. The Elector had to cough up 100,000 to his minister, in installments. Despite the building costs, that was a handsome profit for Wackerbarth. Now comes the mysterious bit. The sale and contract were kept secret. Publicly, Wackerbarth remained the owner, one can but speculate why. Possibly the Elector, who

1412 First definite mention of the place and manor house, thereafter changes of ownership.

1719 After being completely destroyed by fire, the manor is bought by Imperial Count August Christoph von Wackerbarth. Building works start on the Friedrichsburg palace and park and the orangerie building (1720/21).

1723 Elector Friedrich August I purchases the estate by secret contract and a second building plan is drawn up.

1726 The transfer to Augustus the Strong becomes official. However, the vast building plans are more than he can afford.

1727 The first festival of the Polish White Eagle Order is celebrated to mark Augustus the Strong's saint's day.

1732 Building works at Groß-sedlitz are halted, so the garden complex remains unfinished. It is 12 hectares in area, as opposed to the planned 96 hectares.

1733 Death of Augustus the Strong. In the reign of his son Friedrich August II, Großsedlitz remains a centrepoint of glittering festivals and celebrations.

1756 During the Seven Years War, the palace temporarily becomes the Prussian headquarters.

After 1763 Repair of war damage.

The »Silent Music«

spent a great deal of money on building, wanted to avoid any criticism. He did not like being criticised anyway. Building works were under way in Pillnitz and Moritzburg hunting palace was also being built. The Taschenberg Palace in Dresden was undergoing alterations. In far-off Wermsdorf a new hunting palace (the Hubertusburg) was being built for his son. And the Zwinger had not been completed.

Not until 1726 was the change of ownership made public. By then, quite a lot of building had gone on, partly at the wishes of and under the influence of Augustus the Strong. Yet again, the plans were on a gigantic scale. But the Elector's coffers did not allow their implementation. The original plans remained incomplete.

Along the avenue of lime trees and then to the entrance gate. Großsedlitz always seems to be resting in a divine peace and quiet, far from busy roads. It is as if its makers had held their breath before inserting this great work into the landscape. The garden sinks into the depths. The upper orangerie and the new Friedrichsschlösschen, a double flight of steps leads to the upper lawned terrace, the bowling green. On stone balustrades, vases with medallions depicting Roman emperors. Flights of stairs link the upper and lower levels. The ground-level lawn is lined with lime trees. Framed in green, fountains spring from elongated canal basins. And beyond the garden, which vanishes into the countryside, climbs the Stille Musik, or Silent Music, a sweeping flight of steps that mounts a slight slope. Opposite the upper orangerie, the woodland cascades lie amidst greenery. In the dark shadow of the foliage and alongside paths stand conserved and restored sandstone sculptures symbolising the gods of antiquity and the four seasons. Winter is an old man, spring a virgin with a wreath of flowers, summer is adorned with everlasting flowers and ears of corn, and autumn is depicted by Bacchus enjoying a grape.

Barockgarten Großsedlitz is regarded as one of Saxony's most inspired Baroque gardens. And despite suffering destruction during the Seven Years war and under Napoleon, its basic structure has been preserved in unadulterated form. The original sandstone figures have also been largely preserved. Art historians know they are from Permoser's school. And as in other Baroque palaces, the most gifted and important architects and sculptors of the Augustan era worked on it: Johann Christoph Knöffel, who produced his first major work at Großsedlitz, the upper orangerie and the palace, Zacharias Longuelune, who as a Frenchman was best acquainted with the French art of landscape gardening, and Matthäus Daniel

1813 The complex suffers further damage when the grounds are the scene of fighting during the War of Liberation from Napoleon.

1831 Saxony adopts its first constitution, the palace and park become state property

1846 The sandstone figures are completed and restored.

1858 Flights of steps and balustrades are renewed, statues mended.

1861–1864 Conversion of the lower orangerie.

1872–1874 After demolition of the destroyed palace, a new side-wing (the present Friedrichs-schlösschen) is built, designed by court architect Bernhard Krüger.

After 1918 The Friedrichs-schlösschen is used for various purposes. Beginning of a phase when efforts are made to restore the garden's original appearance in meticulous detail. This work continues into the 1930s.

1968–1970 The Friedrichs-schlösschen's original Baroque colour scheme is restored.

Since 1993 Barockgarten Groß-sedlitz has been a state-owned castle enterprise.

The orangerie gardens in morning mood

Pöppelmann, who was mainly involved in the planning of Großsedlitz. Barockgarten Großsedlitz had a privileged place in the Augustan age. As King of Poland, Augustus the Strong had founded the Order of the White Eagle.

On his saint's day, he awarded it to both friends and enemies. A great celebration was held each year to show the Poles that the Germans could hold their drink as well, and be a match for Bacchus. When the flowers bloom in summer and the clipped lime trees stand very still, when concerts are held outside the orangerie whose sounds rise into the lime trees and white beeches, fall on dark statues and get lost in the hills, one is grateful to the makers and all those who preserved this garden true to the original early 18th-century model.

The Friedrichsschlösschen

A fictitious wedding ceremony

August II's love of fun and games found fertile soil among his retainers, too. Indeed, their high spirits sometimes got out of hand, as the following case taken from the court records demonstrates.

On 10 July 1728, when Her Royal Highness Crown Princess Maria Josepha, wife of the future Friedrich August III, Elector of Saxony and King of Poland, was staying in Großsedlitz with her retinue, a certain Margarethe Plutau, daughter of a Swedish soldier and a women from Weesenstein, was staying in the village. Many domestics and courtiers had assembled at the home of Gutjahr the stocking-maker for a merry orgy of eating and drinking. The Plutau woman, a woman of easy virtue, was there too. The others played a joke on her and made her believe that Joseph, Count von Wallenstein's runner, wanted to marry her, but that she had to make up her mind quickly. Margarethe was not disinclined; Joseph offered her his hand and the hunter of the court master of ceremonies was made out to be the bridegroom's father. He gave his consent straight away. The lackey of the master of ceremonies of some countess was elected to join them in wedlock and pretended to be a Master of Theology. He was hastily dressed up accordingly, whereupon he performed the ceremony on the spot, but with the words: »In the name of the cuckoo, the peewit and the great double-bass.« When word got out of this blasphemy and investigations were conducted, the Plutau woman denied that these words had been used. She affirmed that she had been properly married but had been deceived as to the person of the minister. Master Bartzsch, the pastor of Dohna, felt moved to lodge a complaint about this with the Superintendent »because the Superintendent might come to hear about the story, since the whole district was talking about the affair.« He added, however, »that none, neither the lackey, nor the runner, nor the female person was still resident in the parish.«

Abendroth, G. A.: Eine fingierte Trauung. In: Großsedlitz mit seinem königlichen Schlosse und Garten. Dresden, 1862, p. 31 ff.

Schloss Weesenstein

Weesenstein – Seat of the nobility and royal palace

On rounding a bend in the narrow Müglitz valley, it is upon you. The palace towers up on two levels, climbing, climbing. And above it a slim, round tower. The trompe l'oeil painting on the facade shimmers linden green. There is a sound of rushing water from the Mühlbach and the Müglitz. This former seat of the nobility, once said to be three hours on horseback from Dresden, has survived the centuries fairly well and is able to prove it. A touch of Gothic, Renaissance, rural Baroque and Classicism, architectural history from seven centuries, strangely mixed and superimposed. The lower and upper castles merge into each other, mutually supporting each other as if they were jointly seeking a firm hold in the semicircular tower bulging from the front. Active efforts saved Schloss Weesenstein from falling into too much disrepair and kept it habitable. For several hundred years it was owned by the Weesenstein line of the Bünau family, who converted it from a castle into a palace.

In 1830, King Anton bought the palace, and it became private property of the house of Wettin. Soon afterwards, Prince Johann declared Weesenstein his favourite residence, little suspecting what awaited him. People say that »Johann of Saxony came to Weesenstein a prince and returned to Dresden a king.« This happened after King Friedrich August II died unexpectedly in 1854. Johann, the seeker of truth and translator of Dante Alighieri's »Divine Comedy,« remained loyal to the palace even as king. The aristocratic seat was elevated into a royal palace, to a secondary residence where even government business was done. Not a year passed in which the royal family did not spend four weeks at Schloss Weesenstein after their summer sojourn in Pillnitz. There, Johann devoted himself to literature, art and jurisprudence

Page 75:
View of the palace

The rock path

1318 First documentary reference to the castle, as »hus Weysinberg,« owned by the burgraves of Dohna.

1406 The von Bünau family become lords of the castle, for more than 350 years.

1504 The first castle chapel is consecrated.

ca. 1575 The lower castle is built, turning the complex into a residential palace.

First half of the 18th century Intensive building projects, including the Baroque palace chapel by Johann Georg Schmidt, trompe l'oeil facade painting.

1772 The palace is sold to Baroness von Uckermann. Alterations are made to the park and the interior; garden wing and stone bridge are built.

1830–1918 The palace is the private property of the Saxon royal family.

1834 Evidence of the first opening to the public.

1838–1873 Schloss Weesenstein is the favourite residence of King Johann of Saxony, the translator of Dante.

1918 The palace and manor are sold to commoners.

1933/34 The Landesverein Sächsischer Heimatschutz, a regional conservation society, acquires palace and park.

1934 The museum is opened.

and enquired about the state of agriculture and the harvest. He also worked on Dante. Weesenstein must have meant a lot to the king and translator, the scholar and linguist. When on journeys he called himself Count von Weesenstein, or he celebrated it in nostalgic mood: »Happy the man who turning his back/ On the city's vain bustle, greets your refuge/ Where in the quiet coolness of the meadows/ His own herd temptingly reveals itself to him.« There is an aura of Johann's ways and influence in the castle museum, in the living-room and study. Not much is original, some things are painstaking replicas, such as the place where Johann worked as a prince. There, too, stands a bust of his beloved and revered Dante.

Across the bridge. Below, a landscaped park, severely laid out paths, geometric circles, bordered by a path and tree-covered slopes. And on the other bank of the Müglitz open parkland. Back to the colourful Renaissance portal, which has been restored. The palace has received a great deal of loving attention in recent decades and continues to do so. Admittedly, looking at the rear elevation facing the garden it becomes clear that the Free State faces years, if not a decade, before the former aristocratic seat in the Müglitz valley is restored to its former glory. But the interior is in good condition and the original leather and paper wall-coverings, the castle's treasure, are taken care of and properly restored. They date from the 18th and 19th centuries. The strips of leather are precious, as are the French panorama wall-coverings depicting scenes from Chinese life. The palace chapel has also been restored.

The palace was built in a peculiar-seeming order. It grew from top to bottom, from the upper palace to the lower Renaissance palace. First came the castle on the rocky promotory, owned by the burgraves of Dohna. After competing

The palace chapel

1942–1945 The palace is used as a place of safe-keeping for parts of the Dresden collections.

1952 The museum is reopened.

1957 Castle and palace are transferred to the Weesenstein local authority. Restoration work is started under the auspices of the Dresden Institute for the Preservation of Historic Monuments.

1985/86 Extensive reconstruction is carried out.

1993 Schloss Weesenstein becomes a state-owned castle enterprise.

1993/94 Newly designed exhibitions in the castle and the lower palace are opened.

1994 After restoration, the palace chapel is re-consecrated.

for many years with the Wettin margraves for power and influence, they lost. Schloss Weesenstein was not only a dwelling, but a business enterprise. Beneath the roofs of the upper castle lay the granaries, and a brewery ensured a supply of beer. Beer is to be brewed again at Schloss Weesenstein. That is one of the ambitious targets to be fulfilled in the coming years. Much of what was hidden has been reclaimed. The granary, it is now known for sure, was once the castle banqueting hall, as recently uncovered figurative frescos in the so-called Monks' Loft prove. The royal palace kitchen has been reactivated and now serves delicious meals.

The palace interior is somewhat confusing. You walk uphill and down again along the rock face walk. In the cellar built in the rock, whose stone walls shimmer brown in the meagre light, you lose all sense of direction. You have to ask a castle guide to find out where you are. The stables and wine cellar are on the fifth floor and the former ice cellar on the sixth. In the lower vault, a story is told about the von Dohna feud. An atonement crucifix found by a tractor-driver while ploughing a few years back, recalls the murder of the burgrave's son Jan von Dohna. The feud, which started off with a box round the ear, ended up with Margrave Wilhelm as victor. He took advantage of the dispute to incorporate the Dohnas' castle into the Wettins' possessions.

View across the classical style winter garden to the palace park

After so much confusion, the park is enticing. On the opposite side of the Müglitz is the wing of the garden pavilion. The palace's long rear elevation, the garden wing, the balustrade with the large sandstone vases. The building's classical lines make it stand out distinctly from the mediaeval walls. Across the bridge to the small garden pavilion. What buildings tower upon the rock! And it seems fortunate that despite all the building, the new always tolerated the old, that the traces of the centuries were not deleted.

King Johann's study (reconstruction)

King Johann of Saxony

The last journey

It is nearly 200 years ago... The tempest whips the trees on the hillside... Steep and sheer, Schloss Weesenstein reaches up into the night. Everything is bathed in darkness. Only one window flickers in the light of a lamp... Up on the wooded hill by the pavilion, two huntsmen look down into the valley. They gaze spellbound into the uncanny light, forgetting what they were planning to do. Their hands are clenched. A streak of lightning flashes with a hiss. Involuntarily, they cross themselves. »All hell is loose.« »The devil is visiting the old man. God protect our soul!«

»I don't believe it. It's only people's talk!« »People's talk is not nonsense.« The lord of the palace was always a clever man. He spent the night poring over learned books. War brought him money and jewellery in abundance. He grew greedy, and eager to multiply his riches. So he became absorbed in magic. He captivated the devil with magic sayings and crazy spells. On stormy nights he came, amid the roar of the storm and the crash of thunder. With soot and sulphur and stench. Since then, everything the old man has undertaken, has succeeded. The gold blazes in heavy chests... And now he's talking with the devil again. »I feel a cold shudder running through my bones. I can hardly believe it!« Come home, comrade. For stag and deer will never move into our trap. The thought of bagging owl and eagle-owl terrifies me...

The night passes. None was ever so terrible. Even on the next day, the raging storm does not let up. The thunder rolls like distant cart-wheels. Streaks of lightning illuminate the wan daylight with their glare. An oppressive silence hangs over the palace... And so the day drags on to evening. Louder rolls the thunder. Eerily roars the storm. The tall trees whimper. Suddenly, a sharp, rhythmic clatter is heard. A vehicle is rumbling up the drive to the palace.

The coach stops outside the great gate. Two gentlemen alight. Their clothes are black, their fingers scrawny. One seems to have a limp. Their faces are pallid. Their eyes glow eerily. Trembling, the gatekeeper announces the visitors. The dogs howl. An owl cries on the palace roof-ridge or in the tall trees. Rats scurry to the gate. Now the strange figures return, between them the lord of the palace, looking decrepit and feverish. The door is opened. The crazy apparition rushes away. The vehicle fades in clouds of fumes and smoke. The lord never returned.

Soon, a whispering and murmuring was heard in the place. Still now, ghostly cries and diabolical laughter echo around the walls. People say he died far from his homeland. But legend knows better. The Prince of Darkness carried him off, it says, and his soul cries in torment.

Zistel, M.: Die letzte Fahrt. In: Heimat-Jugendblätter zur Heimatkunde für Sächsische Schweiz und Osterzgebirge. No place of publication, 1930, p. 22.

Schloss Moritzburg

A song of praise to hunting: the palace of Moritzburg

Moritzburg hunting palace. What a panorama! Baroque yellow beneath the open sky. Monumental round towers. Balustrade-lined drives lead to the entrances. Weather-vanes follow the wind. Elevations protrude and recede. Cherubs gaze in amazement. Picadors blow hunting horns. Nearing the terrace, the view widens out, revealing a cultivated landscape of tranquil beauty, shaped over centuries and preserved until the present day. Pavilions are reflected in the silky water of ponds. Paths lead into the darkness of deciduous woods. With luck, one encounters a rider on a thoroughbred horse. And one effortlessly starts to picture festivals and hunting parties. Horns sound, packs of dogs chase the game until it is exhausted and is dealt the death-blow.

The Moritzburg region of lakes and forests was a favourite hunting preserve for the Wettin dukes and electors from very early times. It was they who ordered the lakes to be dug. Most are fed by rainwater. On high days and holidays, the kitchen of the royal palace in Dresden served game from the woods, pheasants from the preserve, carp from the ponds. Is it any wonder that inside the palace a song of praise to Baroque life is sung, that the hunt is depicted, and that Diana the goddess of hunting is worshipped? In bygone days, the palace was occasionally referred to as Dianaburg, or Diana's Castle. The nobility loved looking up at allegories, which boosted their self-esteem and encouraged them to make high-handed decisions.

The palace interior opens up like a precious old book, providing testimony to passionate collecting and the Baroque concept of time. Paintings and portraits in ornate frames. Europe's most important collection of antlers is housed in the pa-

Page 83:
A view of the palace

The billiard hall

1542–1546 During the rule of Duke Moritz of Saxony, a Renaissance house is built as a hunting lodge. It is designed by architects Hans von Dehn-Rothfelser and Caspar Voigt von Wierandt. The first hunting lodge is furnished with 30 sets of antlers.

1549 The name »Moritzburch« appears for the first time in documents.

1550 The palace is the administrative headquarters of the newly founded district of Moritzburg.

1584 Under Elector August, alterations by Paul Buchner and Peter Kummer are completed.

1656–1672 Energetic building activity under the supervision of Ezechiel Eckhardt, later of his grandson Johann Albrecht Eckhardt and Wolf Caspar von Klengel; among other things, building of the spiral staircase tower, the chapel lake, the drawbridge, kitchen, bakery, dining-room and »Huntsman's Tower.«

1661–1672 Under Elector Johann Georg II of Saxony, building of the Protestant palace church to plans by Klengel. Ceiling paintings by chief court painter Johann Fink.

1697 As King August II of Poland, Augustus the Strong converts to Catholicism.

1699 The palace chapel is consecrated as a Catholic place of worship.

1703 Plans to alter the hunting lodge, instigated by Augustus the Strong.

lace. The most famous example is the 66-ender, although modern ways of measuring credit it with only 24 tips. At that time, to reach the high figure every minor protuberance was included. That has been corrected, but the legend lives on. This particular set of antlers is one of the few whose origin is known. Elector Friedrich III of Brandenburg killed the stag. Friedrich Wilhelm gave the antlers to Augustus the Strong, builder of the present-day hunting palace, as a present. As a joke, the Brandenburg ruler is said to have asked for a beautiful Saxon youth for personal company. It is not known whether or not his request was granted.

The design of the palace's major apartments is unmistakable. The Baroque furniture and the valuable leather wall-coverings are well worth seeing. The Dresden court's best interior architects and artists were involved in designing Moritzburg: Raymond Leplat as interior designer, Louis de Silvestre as Friedrich August's personal and court painter, and Lorenzo Rossi as painter of wall-coverings.

The hunting palace is named after Moritz, the first Albertinian ruler, who brought the electorate to Dresden for his line. He must have been attracted by the game-rich Friedewald. He had the original building, a manor house with Renaissance gables, defensive walls and towers, erected »on a tongue of land between two lakes.« Other rulers followed suit. Johann Georg II sent his architect Wolf Caspar von Klengel to Moritzburg to add a chapel to the palace. The chapel has remained essentially unaltered. Schloss Moritzburg acquired its present form in the Augustan era. And again it was the cream of craftsmen who put Augustus the Strong's plans into practice: Matthäus Daniel Pöppelmann and the Frenchman Zacharias Longuelune. Friedrich August did not live to see the palace's redesign completed. He died in 1733. Augustus the Strong was followed by two more builders who

The stone hall

discovered and modified this wonderful lake and forest landscape. But the hunting-palace structure was left untouched.

By about 1770, the loud Baroque style was on the decline. The princely rulers were increasingly coming under criticism from English and French Enlightenment thinkers. The greatest upheaval in the 18th century, the French Revolution, was rearing its head. Princes and courts withdrew behind more modest facades. They no longer preferred to spend their time in large palaces, but in salons and garden chateaux. This change can be traced in the Moritzburg countryside, too. From the banqueting hall, the eye follows an elongated corridor stretching into the distance. At the end of this escape route rests a delicately proportioned building, the Fasanen-

1723–1733 The old Renaissance building is converted into a hunting and summer palace. A new zoological garden is laid out under the guidance of chief state architect Matthäus Daniel Pöppelmann.

1725 Many sets of antlers are brought from Schloss Augustusburg to Moritzburg (mainly elk and reindeer antlers, large red-deer antlers and several monster antlers) to furnish the palace halls. In the dining-hall: the world's biggest set of red-deer antlers, an uneven 24-ender rated at 287.5 points.

General view of the castle and outbuildings

From 1727 The interior furnishing of the hunting palace begins: delivery of Saxon leather chairs, writing cabinets, »deersfoot« tables, chests of drawers and other furniture. The palace is decorated with leather wall-coverings (three types: wall-coverings painted with figures in the antler and billiard room, which look almost like tapestries; ornamental wall-coverings pressed with wooden models; iron-punched wall-coverings, also decorated with ornaments). The collection of paintings is enlarged.

1769–ca.1800 Features such as the harbour, the mole and lighthouse, artificial islands, are added.

schlösschen (Small Pheasant Castle). Whereas Moritzburg hunting palace is all weightiness and Baroque show, an abundance of power in architectural form, the Fasanenschlösschen emphasises an elevated bourgeois way of life with courtly ingredients. Late Rococo style is discernible, with oval windows, external staircases and sculptures in quiet poses. Inside, a favourite theme was returned to in some of the rooms. Chinoiserie, the vision of the Far-Eastern art of living, made an appearance, as it had decades previously in Pillnitz and in the Japanese Palace in Dresden's Neustadt. Now very faded and worn, it is to be restored and reclaimed.

The Wettins continued building in the Moritzburg preserve for 250 years. In the beginning was the manor house with the lighthouse at its end. Courtly architecture had run out of

The lighthouse and the Fasanenschlösschen

ideas, but Moritzburg was lucky. Most of the buildings produced since Klengel's day survived. Despite all the worries that old buildings can cause, the palace is planned to rise even higher in its fans' favour. Once, princes and their chosen few celebrated on its terrace and in its halls. Maria Aurora von Königsmarck, Augustus the Strong's first mistress, is said to have been seduced there by the young Elector Friedrich August I. Recently, the rooms have been used for wedding parties and prestigious corporate events. That closes the circle begun by the once modest manor house back in 1546. Palaces have to be used: that is their primary purpose.

1770 The »New Palace« (later the Fasanenschlösschen) is built in the Fasanengarten or Pheasant Garden. Elector Friedrich August III commissions the architect Johann Daniel Schade to design it.

1924–1945 Moritzburg is a residence and museum of the Wettins. Extensive building works are carried out on the palace.

1945 Expropriation as a result of land reform.

1946/47 A Baroque museum is established.

1985–1989 Restoration of the palace chapel.

Since 1993 Moritzburg has been a state-owned castle enterprise.

The court jester Joseph Fröhlich and Augustus the Strong

Joseph Fröhlich (1694–1757) had four different professions: miller, mill engineer, dentist and court jester. Before coming to the Dresden court in 1727, he was the elector's court jester in Bayreuth. In 1756 he had the Narrenhäusel (Fool's House) built for himself in Dresden's Neustadt. Like the building it was modelled on, it had four towers, earning it the nickname »Little Moritzburg.« One day, the following events took place.

Augustus the Strong and his court were on the way to Moritzburg. Joseph Fröhlich had fallen into disfavour and was locked up. He succeeded in outwitting his guard and, along with the court jester and postmaster Schmiedel, set out for Moritzburg to surprise the king. The two of them overtook the court cavalcade and arrived before the king. Standing on ladders, they mischievously welcomed the king across the walls of the state stables office. Augustus was amused by this prank and thereupon ordered two stone busts of them to be made. Later, a building (shed) was erected on the spot, and still today the court jesters' effigies look down from the roof of the Saxony state stud farm in Moritzburg.

Cf. Willnau, C.: Joseph Fröhlich, Hofnarr Augusts des Starken ... In: Mitteilungen des Landesvereins Sächsischer Heimatschutz, Dresden, 1940. Issues 1–4, p. 60 ff.

Albrechtsburg Meissen

Meißen's crown: the Albrechtsburg

High above Meißen tower the Cathedral and the Late Gothic Albrechtsburg, a harmony of stone and light, a crown above the Elbe valley. Saxony's earliest history began here in the land of the Slavic Daleminzi tribe. With the sure eye of a military officer, King Heinrich I had a fort built on top of the rocky cliff overlooking the river. The bishop and chronicler Thietmar von Merseburg, who had seen Meißen with his own eyes, reported in 1018: »King Heinrich cleared a thickly-wooded hill by the Elbe, built a castle there and named it Misni after a stream flowing by on its north side…« When the Wettins rose to be margraves, the castle became more significant to them. In fact, it became the base from which they built up their dynastic power. And so the castle became the cradle of Saxony, although its present appearance did not come till later.

Sometimes, history is unable to get by without irony. Elector Ernst and Duke Albrecht, rulers of Thuringia and Saxony, planned to keep court and rule jointly in Meißen. The two brothers swore to do so for as long as they lived. Saxony was to prosper under their rule, Meißen to be the centre of their power. There they planned to live and there they planned to demonstrate to the German princes the wealth and glory of the House of Wettin. The two brothers found a superb architect, Arnold von Westfalen. Italian Renaissance architecture had not yet spread to the north. Arnold von Westfalen built in late Gothic style, carrying the sandstone sleekly heavenward, creating clearly defined spaces. Unfortunately, he was unable to complete his work. He died in 1482, three years before a momentous day in Saxony's history, the division of the Wettin territories into Ernestinian and Albertinian parts. What had once been sworn was long forgotten. The castle, still not com-

Page 91: Winding stairs in the great staircase tower

A view of the courtyard at night

929 After the German King Heinrich I had overthrown the Daleminzi, he built a castle as a base for German rule in the central Elbe region.

968 Founding of the episcopate of Meißen, first report of a margrave of Meißen.

10th/11th century Energetic building activity in the castle, battles for the castle.

From 1068 Burgraves directly subordinate to the Emperor are appointed, leading to a three-way division of power on the castle hill.

1089 Heinrich I von Eilenburg is the first Wettin to be invested as the March of Meißen.

1123–1125 Konrad the Great establishes long-term Wettin power in the March of Meißen.

1470/71 Arnold von Westfalen is appointed Saxony's chief architect. Building starts of the Albrechtburg as a residence for the joint rulers and brothers Ernst and Albrecht.

1489 Provisional completion of the castle by von Westfalen's successor (from 1482), Conrad Pflüger. Because the state was divided in 1485, the castle was never used as an official royal residence.

1521–1524 The castle is completed under Duke George the Bearded.

1645 In the Thirty Years War, Meißen is taken by Swedish troops. After storming the castle

pletely finished, lost its purpose. Nearby Dresden was elevated into the permanent royal seat of the Albertinians, while the Ernestinians resided in Wittenberg and later in Torgau. Soon, however, posterity agreed that Arnold von Westfalen had created an epoch-making work of architecture that was completed by his successors. He broke with conventional German castle architecture and its defensive function and founded a new school whose primary purpose was to impress.

Enter the castle and cathedral precinct. The wonder of a place of which one senses the beauty. The hexagonal great winding staircase on the castle's courtyard facade, delicately proportioned stones dividing up cell-vaulted galleries, cornices horizontally defining and separating the floors, the gable windows – finest Gothic speaks quietly. Atop the fourth floor of the spiral staircase, the tall conical roof. It was not built by Arnold von Westfalen, but added in the 19th century. However, the Saxon state architect is said to have invented the recessed arched window.

Since 1676, the castled has borne Albrecht's name. Otherwise, however, the Wettins did not have much use for it. It never became a seat of government. In the early 18th century, the Albrechtsburg suffered a strange fate. A charlatan, an apothecary who claimed he could make gold, had succeeded firing porcelain in the casemates at Dresden. Johann Friedrich Böttger kept his master, Elector Augustus the Strong, waiting for eight years before giving him porcelain instead of gold. But it was worth its weight in gold, because porcelain came from far-off places, from Asia, Japan and China. In January 1710 the Elector published a manifesto announcing the discovery of European porcelain, but without mentioning Böttger's name, presumably as a precaution and out of mistrust. For it could not be ruled out that attempts might be made to abduct the man or lure him away. Augustus the Strong had done that himself years before when he had Böttger brought to Saxony. The Elector needed a safe, easily-guarded place for the future production facility, for the kilns, for storing the valuable kaolin, for the mixture itself. The Albrechtsburg seemed suitable. It could be very well guarded. In 1710 the Elector ordered a factory to be set up in the castle rooms. For 153 years, the porcelain with the blue swords logo was fired and shaped there. That was not good for the old building. People began to feel a sense of responsibility for Westfalen's masterpiece. Finally, the factory moved to a new building in the Triebisch valley where the state porcelain factory is still located now.

Into the castle. Coolness. Walk reverently across old stones. Ribbed, cell-like stellar vaulting in its storeys, suppor-

hill, they completely destroy the palace interior.

1676 After restoration, by order of Johann Georg II, the palace is named Albrechtsburg.

1710 Europe's first porcelain factory is established in the Meissen Albrechtsburg. Böttger is its first administrator, until his death in 1719.

1863 The factory is shifted to the new premises in the Triebisch valley, and reconstruction of the castle begins.

1873 The rooms begin to be decorated with large epic paintings and large-scale ornamentation in the historicist style.

The Great Appeals Room

The castle hill

1881 Opening as a memorial to Saxon history.

1902–1908 The cathedral building is completed by the addition of two west towers.

ted on beautifully proportioned clustered pillars, the Great Court Room and the Small Dining Room, the Great Appeals Room. Nineteenth-century wall-paintings illustrate the ancient history of the Meißen castle and Saxony, somewhat majestically and heroically, in the pictorial language of the 19th century. Heinrich I founding the castle, the arrival of the

Wettin prince Konrad the Great in Meißen in 1125, portraits of margraves, Emperor Friedrich III investing Ernst and Albrecht of Saxony and Thuringia, Albrecht at the age of six being betrothed in Eger to Zedena, the nine-year-old daughter of the King of Bohemia. Glorious history, understood in the context of its period, is shown here as being colourful and significant. The development of the land of the Wettins, which began with the investiture of the first Wettin in 1089, becomes imaginable, high quality late-Gothic architecture, a piece of German history that all began with the building of the castle in the country of the West Slavic Daleminzi.

1939–1945 Works of art from various museums and from the Meissen porcelain factory are stored for safe keeping.

1963–1970 Extensive restoration work is carried out.

1990 The Free State of Saxony is founded with a formal ceremony in the Albrechtsburg.

Since 1993 The Albrechstburg Meissen has been a state-owned castle enterprise.

The Thirty Years War – an eye-witness report

»An explosion in the 10 windows, so everyone goes into the palace courtyard, and one of these windows hits Stichen on the neck. He fell to the ground and lay so still that I couldn't help thinking he was dead. Only after briefly getting over the fright, he got up and ran off, but he looked strange, because he had the window-frame across his neck like a yoke.

This grenade explosion threw glass from the window into the face of a girl, Magdalena Sattlerin, so that she was very bloody and wounded. Soon the enemy threw some more fire grenades onto the floor of the administrative building, which with such a terrible, dreadful explosion almost like a thunder-clap knocked several thousand, indeed all the tiles from the administrative building roof, with such great rattling that we could no longer hear or see anything, but praise be to God nobody was injured and nothing caught fire. Only we did not feel like tarrying too long, so we abandoned our food and drink and hid in a large underground vault in the palace. As we started to flee, another grenade fell into the administrative building, with such force that it tore the wooden spiral staircase that goes up to the roof away from the building and smashed it as if it had never been. And on this day 10 of this type of grenade and many stones were thrown in, though little damage was done in other places, except that several sheep that were walking in the palace courtyard were killed.

On Thursday, 14 August 1645, at 5 a.m. the enemy began to fire cannon dreadfully and mightily, and to shoot at Kornschreiber's clubhouse next to the fortress, also occasionally to throw powerful grenades, so that it wasn't safe anywhere. But because I badly wanted to know what was happening with the storming, I went into the vaulted dining-room, in which 15 to 20 musketeers with double-edged hatchets and muskets lay in the fortifications by the Lommatzsch Gate to stop the enemy from running at the press, and after several of the enemy approached the press, they gave them such a reception that they went tumbling down the hill.«

Handwritten text, author unknown.

Schloss Nossen

A bright Renaissance palace in Nossen

This happy place certainly has something to boast of. In the middle of the small town of Nossen and over its roofs towers an imposing palace. Those who want to see and experience it are rewarded – with gentle countryside, with stories of bygone ages and with the certainty that the Free State of Saxony takes care of its heritage. Especially since German reunification, the palace has set out to tell its story in detail, including how the district of Nossen developed.

Walking from the market past the parish church, the palace towers above the left bank of the Freiberg Mulde. The whitish-grey of the facade, the red of the roof-tiles, the semi-circular towers facing the moat. It took more than ten years to restore the buildings to their former glory. Across the arched bridge, through the shadow of the plain portal, into the courtyard. An amiable place. White clover amidst the green of the lawn, lilac bushes. Gables, windows and towers. And from the edge of the courtyard the town displays its colourful, sloping roofs. This palace is still lived in.

One should take ones time, for time has passed through this small town. Great history did not take place here. Citizens who farmed land lived in the town. Modesty was native to Nossen, and there was often more worry than joy when the harvests were meagre. Perhaps the craftsmen and farmers even sympathised with Böttcher Eckold, the comrade-in-arms of Lips Tullian. Eckold, who with Tullian's band struck fear and terror into the wealthy, was locked in the palace dungeon awaiting execution. He had helped himself to what was denied to ordinary citizens. Legend tells attractively embellished stories about the nobility of this band, who shared their booty with the poor.

Page 99:
The palace's south-west wing seen from Rodigt

The castle and town came into being on the border between country long settled by Slavs and the dark, richly-

The 16th-century west wing

wooded Erzgebirge mountain region. The bishops of Meißen made a grab for the place early on. Even clergymen felt the urge for land and possessions, influence and power.

Did the knightly family that owned the castle give up too quickly because it was no match for Meißen? Or did it just decide to take the money and go, when the churchmen offered cash for the castle and the small district? We will never know. However, there is documentary evidence that by about 1315 the bishop was the owner. The episcopate of Meißen, Saxony's mini-Rome, had gained another sinecure. The palace grounds and the accompanying possessions aroused covetous desires later on, too. In 1436, 121 years later, the Monastery of Altzella bought the palace and its extensive estates. When the Reformation and Lutheran doctrine gained hold of the flat countryside and the monastery was secularised, the era of the monks came to an end. The palace passed into secular ownership and took over the district of Nossen. Evidently, Elector August did not like the look of the building where the court occasionally stayed, and had it extended in Renaissance style.

1185 The first appearance of a nobleman von Nossen as owner of the Nossen castle district.

1268 First mention of the castle, as »castrum Nvzin.«

1316–1403 Schloss Nossen is owned directly by the bishops of Meißen. The castle is extended and converted into a palace.

1403–1436 The land and buildings are rented or leased to various people.

1436 Altzella Monastery buys Schloss Nossen for 4,200 florins. The monastery abbots often stayed at the palace, or used it as their official residence.

1540 As a consequence of the Reformation in Saxony, the monastery is secularised (confiscated and declared state property).

1544 The palace becomes the headquarters of the new electoral district of Nossen.

1554–1557 Elector August has the Renaissance-style west wing (hall) built of demolition material from Altzella. With the gigantic hall, the court parlour and the apartments, it serves the Elector's court as a hunting and travel lodge.

1628–1630 The south wing is built as an office for the district governor.

1646 All the living quarters are devastated as a result of the Thirty Years War.

1667–1669 The north-west wing is redesigned (kitchen building) and remnants of the old castle removed, under the supervision of Wolf Caspar von Klengel.

1712 Böttcher Eckold, a member of Lips Tullian's notorious band of robbers, is held prisoner at the palace prior to execution.

1716 Countess Cosel spends a month as a prisoner in the palace before being transferred to the fortress of Stolpen.

1775 The palace is abandoned as an electoral residence. Thereafter, it is used by various government offices (e.g. the finance office, the justice department, the treasury), and altered accordingly.

1813 Napoleon spends the night at the palace, his soldiers ransack the town.

1857 The hall building is renewed under the supervision of Carl Moritz Haenel.

Since 1877 The palace is used for a variety of purposes (prison, approved school).

1907 After extensive alterations, the Renaissance-period coffered ceiling from the deanery is taken to the Dresden Arts and Crafts Museum.

1952 The Nossen District Court moves out, and the palace is used mainly as living quarters.

Local history museum

A major building phase began, one that shaped the palace to its present form. After August's death, the Wettins used Schloss Nossen (Nossen Castle) less frequently. They did not lose sight of it, however. They hunted in the Nossen woods and kept the palace intact as a travel lodge. An exhibition in the light rooms of the newly designed museum tells the story in pictures and figures. And anyone who wants to delve into the history of the district of Nossen can do so, thanks to a new exhibition.

Schloss Nossen boasts two events of note, one of them military and the other associated with a woman's fate. It is 23 November 1716. An escort arrives at the palace. In the carriage sits Countess Cosel. Prussia, to which she had fled, has extradited her at the request of Augustus the Strong. Not for nothing, though. The Elector of Saxony paid by returning Prussian deserters who had fled from Brandenburg. A fine deal by honourable monarchs. Countess Cosel is strictly guarded. On the journey, she has fainted several times. The men treat her roughly. She is a prisoner. In Merseburg she was even raped.

It is cold in the palace. The long journey and despair have weakened Mistress Cosel, Friedrich August I's glamorous mistress. She suffers a stroke. An eye-witness report says: »She is so wretched that it would move a stone to pity.« On 24 December, the once-feted countess, still sick, is laid in the carriage. She is too weak to sit up. She has no idea where she is being taken. The destination is Stolpen Castle. That is what Augustus the Strong has ordered. There, she can be well guarded. And so begins a sad story of princely despotism devoid of mercy.

The other event that made Nossen well-known was that Napoleon used it as his headquarters on the eve of the battle for Dresden. Here, on 7 May 1813, he planned the storming of the Saxon capital, which was held by the Allies. From here he issued the last orders that gave him the military upper hand once more, before his defeat at the Battle of the Nations at Leipzig. After heavy fighting, Dresden was captured.

Leave the palace walls and go up to the ruined monastery of Altzella, which was no match for the ravages of time.

1954–1985 The Nossen Local History Museum, founded in 1905, moves into the west wing. It has to be closed when repairs become essential.

1981–1990 The palace is reconstructed in the context of a housing modernisation project.

Since 1993 Schloss Nossen, together with Altzella monastery park, has been a state-owned castle enterprise.

The ghost of Nossen hill

On the footpath leading up the south side of the castle hill from the lower town (or the »hole,« as people used to call it) to the upper town, as recently as 50 years ago a ghost known as the Schamprich used to get up to his tricks. At night, he would jump on the backs of people starting out along the path and ride piggy-back uphill as far as the stump of a large oak-tree, growing heavier and heavier. He disappeared when the new Dresden road was built and the upper section of the path was abandoned. The oak-tree stump was opposite the palace's thick, round, corner tower to the left of the path, in which the notorious church-robber Lips Tullian is said to have been imprisoned for some time. In former times the town's night watchman had to walk along the palace's north moat and sound the hours from the outermost corner of the hill, by the so-called deanery. One winter's night, an invisible hand boxed him round the ears, sending his fur cap rolling downhill. He blamed this prank on the Schamprich.

Quoted from Meiche, A.: Sagenbuch des Königreichs Sachsen. Leipzig, 1903, p. 141

Klosterpark Altzella

Altzella, the monastery ruin beneath cool canopies of leaves

Page 105: Mausoleum

The ruined monastery of Altzella near Nossen is hidden behind a high wall of undressed stone. Shrouded in mystery, imbued with the mediaeval past. Nearby flows the Freiberg Mulde. Those who want to enjoy the ruins, which merge with the park into one large, sentimental painting, for longer should take their time before entering the monastery precinct. The path by the stone wall is lined with cherry and apple trees. In spring the place bursts with blossom, and in autumn a fire of colours sparkles. Summer filters more coolly through the canopy of leaves. And in winter, the field of ruins is revealed, showing all its vulnerability to time and human destruction.

Prayer column in the monastery park

During the Reformation, when ancient altars were stormed in many places and effigies of saints went up in flames, the monastery too suffered damage. Its doors were closed in 1540. The Cistercian monks converted to the new Christian doctrine or moved away. The buildings were devoid of protection. The collegiate church was demolished, walls tumbled down. Not infrequently, citizens of nearby Nossen built their houses from the monastery stones. The Renaissance palace of Nossen was also built with stones from the monastery. The town church's two portals come from the refectory, the dining-room and the Altzella chapter room. Despite everything, this was fortunate, because it meant that Cistercian architecture was preserved elsewhere. Some things survived in the monastery precinct, and have for some time been paid the respect that was lacking for centuries.

No bell hangs by the entrance, no Cistercian monk asks you to step inside. In the park, ancient beech and lime trees rustle, clearings open up. In the shadows and beneath the treetops there are walls and arches, remains of the summer re-

Inside the mausoleum

fectory and the abbey overgrown with ferns and the mausoleum, which was built later. This area has repeatedly attracted painters, among them Caspar David Friedrich and Adrian Ludwig Richter. The result was songs in colour. The monastery was built on 800 acres of newly cleared land. Emperor Friedrich I transferred it to the Margraves of Meißen. Previously, the Wettin Margrave Otto the Rich, who was to make his fortune from Freiberg silver, had founded an abbey. Otto was a generous donor and gave the monastery some land in the Freiberg area itself. The gift was not entirely altruistic, however. The Cistercians were seen as experienced monastery-founders, and Otto the Rich was thinking about his death. He wanted a tomb for himself and his wife, Hedwig, in the monastery. The monks were pleased with the gift, but their joy proved to be short-lived when silver ore was discovered not

1162 Emperor Friedrich I transfers 800 acres of cleared land to Margrave Otto of Meißen, for an abbey founded by the latter.

1175 The abbot and his convent move from the Cistercian monastery of Pforte (Naumburg) to the monastery of Cella.

From 1175 The monastery church is built.

1180–1230 Proof of energetic building activity. The buildings in the closed area and the Romanesque stepped portal are erected.

1190–1381 Cella Monastery is the burial place of the house of Wettin.

1198 Consecration of the monastery church, a brick building with a nave, two side aisles and a transept. North Italian influence is still visible in the west front.

1268 A daughter monastery, Neuzella, is founded near Guben. Gradually, the name Cella Vetus (Old Cella, or in German Altzella), becomes established.

14th and 15th century The monastery experiences its heyday under Abbot Vinzenz von Gruner and Abbot Martin von Lochau.

1436 The monastery purchases Nossen palace for 4,200 florins, complete with contents and land. The palace buildings are in poor repair. It is converted into an official residence for the abbot.

1501–1522 The humanist Martin von Lochau serves as abbot.

1506 The upper floor of the lay brothers' building is converted into a library.

1540 Secularisation (seizure of the monastery as a result of the Reformation in Saxony). The last abbot leases the business part of the monastery.

1543 The monastery library is taken over by Leipzig University library.

Until 1555 The monastery remains the administrative headquarters for the former estates and possessions.

1553–1586 Elector August grants permission for the monastery to be used for building material, the contents are given away.

1676 Elector Johann Georg II orders excavations in the vicinity of the church and high altar, in search of the bones of his ancestors.

1676–1680 Head state architect, Wolf Caspar von Klengel, designs a mausoleum, but it remains unfinished.

ca. 1700 The dining-room of the lay brothers' building becomes a cow byre, the library and the loft are turned into grain stores.

1787–1804 The burial chapel is converted into a conventional mausoleum, the monastery ruins are incorporated into the design of a romantic landscaped park.

Remains of the monastery

far below the ground in Freiberg. A great mining rush began. And Otto, in return for compensation, took back his gift. No doubt the Cistercian order grumbled, but the Margrave's hand was stronger. Nonetheless, the monastery flourished. In 1175, the convent moved in. The monks came from Pforte near Naumburg. No, the order was certainly not poor, for large-scale building activity started scarcely five years later. The Romanesque stepped portal, the main entrance, the lay brothers' building, the cloister and the church all appeared. The Cistercians single-mindedly multiplied their possessions, even establishing a monastery farm above the bank of the Elbe in Zadel. In Dresden, Zellescher Weg still commemorates their astute dealings. The monks were industrious and efficiently got people to work for the monastery. According to the rules of their order, the monks busied themselves with books, prayer and the word of God, so they had too little time for practical work, which was done by lay brothers. The stores filled with grain, which earned them good money.

The open expanse of the monastery precinct has a wide-spread appearance. The granary gables are touched with bright light, the rooms open to the sky. To the left is the lay brothers' building, which has defied the ravages of time more successfully. Here, one gains an idea of monastery life. A wine-cellar and brewery can be made out. The men of God did not spend all their time praying. The people of Franconia, who had cleared the forest long before, surely brought the grape-vine with them.

Soon, Altzella Monastery developed into an intellectual centre for the margravate of Meißen. A substantial library brought together the knowledge of the day. And when Luther's call came from Wittenberg, the monastery opposed the Reformer. In vain.

The lay brothers' building, in which they dined and slept, is an experience, with its mighty saddle roof and imposing, newly rendered, long front. In the refectory cloister, one can experience Cistercian architecture, plain pillars with ornate capitals. The exterior of the lay brothers' building has been largely renovated and restored. The former library hall is accessible once more, and the spiral staircase has been reconstructed. That which was destroyed by human hand is being reclaimed at great expense. An exhibition tells the story. The monastery ruin is being paid the respect that befits it. But perhaps one of the greatest experiences is the way a garden designer has arranged ruins and trees into a park that is both romantic and sentimental, a landscape of the type beloved of Romantic painters and copper-etchers, with trees and clouds, mist patches and flooding moonlight.

18th/19th century Altzella serves as a backdrop (for drawings and paintings) for Dresden artists such as Johann Christian Klengel, Johann Gottfried Klinsky, Christian August Günther, Caspar David Friedrich, Adrian Ludwig Richter and Otto Wagner.

ca. 1800 The garden artist Hübner begins designing his romantic landscaped park. Demolition works take place and building rubble is cleared. Axes of view are arranged to incorporate architectural remains of the Romanesque buildings.

Post-1945 to 1990 Used as a nationalised estate, falls into further decay.

1953–1962 Investigations by the Institute for the Preservation of Historic Monuments, Dresden.

1955–1961 The gem collection is housed in the former dining-room.

Since 1990 Extensive repair and renovation works.

1993 Altzella Monastery Park, together with Schloss Nossen, becomes a state-owned castle enterprise.

1994 The mausoleum is reconsecrated.

The Altzella monastery robber

The annals of Petersberg (Lautenberg) and Altenzella refer to Margrave Albrecht, who ruled from 1190 to 1195, as »The Proud,« but also »The Arrogant.« The latter epithet recalled his high-handed actions against the monasteries, which earned him reproach from the chroniclers. Indeed, a contemptuous act that he performed against the monastery of Altzella (near Nossen) is reported. His father, Margrave Otto the Rich, had deposited three thousand marks in silver with the monastery. The monks claimed it was to be used for saying masses for his eternal salvation. Albrecht doubted this purpose and demanded that the abbot return the money. The monks objected, but in vain. Finally, when pleas and arguments proved to no avail, they placed the money on the altar of the Virgin Mary. Would the new Margrave, in his lust for money, dare to remove the hoard that had been placed under the protection of the Holy Virgin? He would! To the monks' great dismay, Albrecht took possession of the money without any inhibitions. That was undoubtedly a very unwise thing to do, for it made him bitter enemies at the time and ensured unfavourable reports for posterity.
As punishment for robbing the church, he is said to have fallen ill and to have smelled so foul that none of his few friends wanted to stay near him. He died in 1195, allegedly after being poisoned by one of his confidants, a man called Hugold.

Cf. Geschichten und Sagen des Meißner Landes, Teil I. Meißen, 1989, p. 19

Ardently courted and fought over by kings and margraves: Burg Mildenstein

Driving along, the countryside glides by. A wide turn. From the A14 autobahn towards Leisnig and Burg Mildenstein (Mildenstein Castle). The forests along the rivers Elbe and Mulde were dense when, in winter 928/29, the Liudolfingian Heinrich I's war hordes invaded Sorbian territory. If their battle was to have been worthwhile, they had to safeguard what they had conquered. After Heinrich's death, the conquerors had experience of this, so they continued what Heinrich had begun. They looked at the tall, narrow rock above the Mulde with a practised eye. The river protected it and from the top, they could see far across the countryside. Orders were given. Plenty of wood was at hand. They felled trees and built a castle. The foundations of a village were laid. Later, a settlement was to adjoin the fortifications, and Leisnig came into being.

The castle is recorded as having been a fortress in 1046. The Salian Emperor Heinrich III signed over several fortresses to his wife, and Leisnig was one of them. The Mulde valley had been annexed to the Frankish-German territories and belonged to the Empire. From that time on, the castle of Leisnig was entrusted only to the most loyal. One of them was Count Wiprecht von Griotzsch, who caused trouble for the Margrave of Meißen. He was an energetic man and strove to increase his landed possessions. What is more, he was a staunch supporter of the central imperial power. When Emperor Heinrich IV, who ate humble pie at Canossa, was excommunicated by the Pope, Wiprecht remained loyal to him. His loyalty was rewarded when Heinrich IV invested him of with Leisnig and other fortresses. Wiprecht became the first great builder. Later, Duke Friedrich III of Swabia, the subsequent Emperor Friedrich Barbarossa, came by the castle,

Page 111:
The manor house

The grain loft

1046 First mention of a lord of the manor of Leisnig.

1084 Emperor Heinrich IV transfers Leisnig Castle to Wiprecht von Groitzsch.

1147 Duke Friedrich III of Swabia, later to become emperor Friedrich Barbarossa, purchases Leisnig as his private property.

1158 By means of a swap, Leisnig becomes property of the Empire, the castle is the seat of a burgrave.

1192 The burgraves of Leisnig found the Buch Monastery.

1365 End of the burgraviate, the margraves of Meißen take possession of the castle and town.

ca. 1400 Lively building activity in the castle (building of the granary).

1485 The castle is the headquarters of an administrative district in the Ernestinian part of Saxony.

1547 The district of Leisnig is allocated to the Leipzig administrative region, responsible for managing the state ruler's landed property, keeping watch on the local aristocracy, registering services, justice and civil jurisprudence.

1632–1645 The castle is repeatedly besieged, bombarded and stormed during the Thirty Years War.

making Leisnig a possession of the Staufen dynasty. When he ceded it to the Empire in return for other possessions, the region around Leisnig became a domain of the Empire. The burgraviate was administered by burgraves appointed by the Emperor. That was not to remain so. The Margraves of Meißen, who were single-mindedly and rigorously expanding their domestic power, had long had their eye on the burgraviate. They wanted it. The Wettins were waiting for an occasion, a suitable opportunity, to step in.

We reach Polkenberg. Leisnig lies in the valley. To the right of the road the Freiberg Mulde flows along at a leisurely pace. Alders and rowanberry trees line its banks. Willows bow to the river. Turning a bend, Mildenstein Castle comes into sight. Amber-coloured walls gleam in the late afternoon light. The castle keep peeps out above the dark roofs. The pages' building looks splendid in its white render.

Approach is imminent.

Along the castle fief, past the outer castle, one sees the white facades of the castle lords' house and pages' building, the ramparts wall and, on the side facing the Mulde, the castle chapel. A great deal of work has been done in recent years. Large sections of the castle have been – at least externally – repaired and renovated. Three elderly ladies sit in the courtyard outside the residential buildings. »It's turned out very nice here, hasn't it? Don't forget to go up into the granary loft. You'll be amazed.«

The present outer castle was built by the Wettins. They had waited doggedly. Their domestic power had increased so that neither emperor nor king could ignore them. Both needed their support, needed them as allies in wars and power blocs. Margrave Friedrich II had attained his first objective in 1329, when Emperor Ludwig IV in far-off Pavia invested him as the Lord of Leisnig. But there already was a lord in Leisnig, even

A view of the castle

though he was now a Wettin vassal. The Wettins wanted to strip him of his power completely. A dispute between the lord and the nearby Cistercian monastery gave them reason to intervene. The lord had destroyed the monastery. The abbot requested the margrave's help. Leisnig was besieged and the lord surrendered. That gave the margraves a free hand. Margrave Wilhelm had the newly acquired castle altered in the Gothic style. Thereafter, the name Mildenstein established itself as the castle's name. Mildenstein, once so ardently courted, gradually lost its defensive character, even a few metres of the keep were demolished. Knightly halls were transformed into offices. Burg Mildenstein, for which people in Dresden had little use in the Augustan era, was converted into an electoral district court. Finally, the history and

1706/07 Stanislav Leszczynski, Augustus the Strong's rival claimant to the Polish throne, chooses the castle as his residence and signs the Peace of Altrandstädt.

1708 Burg Mildenstein is used as the elector's district court, as a prison, and as civil servants' dwellings.

1871–1875 The castle keep is restored by the Leisnig history and antiquity society. The keep is extended into a viewing tower.

1890 The local history museum is established in the castle.

General view of the castle and outbuildings

1953 The municipal local history museum is expanded into a county museum.

1993 Burg Mildenstein becomes a state-owned castle enterprise of the Free State of Saxony.

antiquity society took an interest in it and arranged some rooms as exhibitions. In 1945, the castle was transferred to the municipality. However, this had little influence on Mildenstein, because it was used as a prison until 1952. Gradually the authorities, pressed by conservationists and local history aficionados, are reminded of the castle's historical value. The museum was expanded, and the castle remains a museum to this day. Weapons are on show here. One room is dedicated to the painter Karl Wagler. And those looking for curiosities will not be disappointed. In the castle, they can see the biggest top-boot in the world, 3.70 metres long. Leisnig shoemakers have meanwhile made a new boot that is said to be one metre longer.

Of late, the public has become more aware of the erstwhile fortress. The castle's St. Martin's chapel, the oldest building in the complex, was restored and radiates its original beauty. The granary loft is truly a masterpiece of carpentry. The large room, spanned with beams that look like a delicately-proportioned vault, is used for exhibitions. Concerts are occasionally held in the chapel, in front of the precious triptych altar that was created by an unknown Late Gothic master around 1500.

The people in charge of the castle have great plans. The collections are to be expanded, and the castle is to be opened for private functions. Back to the ramparts wall. A roar rises from the valley, the sound of a train whose tracks follow the course of the Mulde. Afterwards, silence falls again. The hills on the other side of the river descend slowly into darkness. In the town, lights are switched on, signs of life in a town that owes its origin to the castle.

The giant top-boot

How Wiprecht fought a lion

For many years, Wiprecht's heroic deeds were a topic of conversation at the Emperor's dining-table. The Archbishops of Mainz and Cologne, the Bishops of Münster and Halberstadt and many other princes and lords praised his heroism and bravery and lauded him as the most fearless fighter under the sun. The Emperor listened to their praise, but remained sceptical. »We shall see whether Wiprecht is so brave when we have put him to the test,« he said. »Bring him here, let's see if he can't be frightened after all.« While Count Wiprecht was being summoned to the Emperor, the latter had an enclosure opened in which a ferocious lion was kept. The lion was given the freedom to have a look around the palace courtyard, which Wiprecht had to cross on his way to the Emperor. Stepping out of its cage, it uttered a frightening roar. The Emperor and all the gentlemen of his retinue hid in safe places from which they could watch the courtyard. The unsuspecting Wiprecht obeyed the Emperor's command. He walked calmly across the courtyard in front of his squire, who was carrying his sword and shield. Scarcely had the lion caught sight of Wiprecht than he pounced on him with a roar. Without hesitating, the squire threw himself into the path of the charging lion. But Wiprecht was not the type to rely on other people's strength. He grabbed the squire, threw him aside and countered the lion's attack with his bare hands. Seizing the lion by its mane, he shook and ruffled the raging animal with such strength that the king of the desert's roar faded into a pathetic whimper. Finally, the lion slunk away with its tail between its legs. Wiprecht went calmly to the Emperor as if nothing had happened and asked what he required. The Emperor smiled benevolently and said: »I require nothing of you. People praised your fearlessness to me and I wanted to test it.« Having told him he had passed the test, the Emperor made to dismiss Wiprecht. But Wiprecht, finding it hard to conceal his anger, barked at the Emperor: »You reward my loyalty badly. I followed you not for idle games, but for serious battle. But I no longer care to serve an emperor who delivers his servants to the mercy of wild animals for his own gratification.« Thus saying, Wiprecht left the ashamed emperor standing, took his shield and sword from his squire and strode proudly away.

Quoted from Walz, D.: Burgetour. Leipzig (Sachsenbuch), 1992, p. 72

Preserved over time: Burg Gnandstein

Kohrener Land, castle country, and the trees are laden with fruit, apples, pears and cherries. Nearby is the old town of Altenburg and the cities of Leipzig and Chemnitz. The desire to travel and curiosity have long set in, with a feeling of gratitude that such quiet, still landscapes exist. Burg Gnandstein (Gnandstein Castle) is the destination. What will it be like? What effect will the castle have, and what tales will it tell? The books say it is one of Saxony's oldest knightly castles, the oldest remaining Romanesque castle in the Pleißenland region, a castle over which emperors, kings and the ambitious and up-and-coming Wettins fiercely argued and fought. The Wettins emerged the victors. And they showed their gratitude to those who had stood by them in the battles of the era, investing the von Einsiedel family as rulers of Gnandstein. They made themselves indispensable to the state rulers, the electors of Saxony and the dukes, and multiplied their own estates. They grew rich, and were soon were one of the most respected families of the Saxon nobility. They chose Gnandstein as their family seat.

Passing Kohren, the road now descends into a lovely valley. Then there it is, the castle, and again, like the others, it rests on a rocky promontory. Walls stretch up toward the sky. Fresh red roof tiles. Scaffolding. The castle is heading for good times. And above pointed gables and roofs towers one espies the castle keep, fortified with battlements. A long facade stretches out. And beneath the castle lies the village. Somebody blows a trumpet, and doves coo in lime and chestnut trees. The only thing missing for courtly love is the lady. But the trumpeter is no troubadour, he is playing for the rattling coins that twinkle in his hat. One passes through the gate, defences and castle courtyard. Ivy entwines itself

Page 119: Looking toward the castle keep

A view of the castle

around the arcades. Tables and chairs promise West Saxon hospitality.

First to the ancestors, the Einsiedels' family gallery, and then to the chapel, which is said to be particularly beautiful. Energetic men look down from oval frames, conscious of their importance in the State of their day. Squeezed into Renaissance armour, in Baroque abundance, bearded and beardless. They understood the sign of their times. Through all the difficult times, Gnandstein remained in their possession until the post-World War II land reform. Only then did they have to give up and leave the east of Germany. The line of ancestors starts with Hildebrand von Einsiedel, who seems to have been a cool calculator and to have had an eye to his own advan-

1228 First recorded mention of the castle, the vassals of the margrave call themselves von Gnandstein.

ca. 1250 the original castle is extended.

1317 Gnandstein is in the possession of the burgraves of Altenburg.

1329 The castle passes by inheritance to the burgraves of Leisnig.

ca. 1350 The complex is extended.

ca. 1400–1939 Burg Gnandstein is owned by the von Einsiedel family.

1485 The Leipzig Division – the border of the divided Wettin territories runs through Gnandstein territory.

Before 1500 Extension of the fortifications; the castle chapel with the three altars (1501–1503) is built with the help of Peter Breuer.

1632 Swedish troops destroy castle buildings.

ca. 1700 Baroque-style alterations to the Gothic south wing and all facades facing the courtyard are carried out.

1812 The chapel wing is redesigned.

ca. 1840 The battlements and the knights' hall are renovated.

1911 The castle keep is opened to the public.

tage. Elector Friedrich entrusted him with mines, the mint, taxes, in fact the state finances in general. Hildebrand is regarded as the founder of the older Einsiedel-Gnandstein line. He knew his way around the silver-rich Erzgebirge mines and profited from them, as did his successors. Next to him his son Heinrich, Privy Councillor to Elector Ernst and Duke Albrecht, the dividers of the Wettin territory. Previously, he had gone to the Holy Land with Wilhelm III, Count of Thuringia, and had been knighted there. It was he who had Gnandstein Castle converted into a residence and established the chapel within its walls.

Art historians divide the castle's building history into several sections. It began in about 1200 and ended at the beginning of the 19th century. The castle grew bigger and taller. Gothic sense of style manifested itself. In the Thirty Years War, the castle did not go unscathed. Swedish troops invaded it and set light to the heated apartments. Lightning and fire destroyed some buildings. They were rebuilt in simple Baroque style. The family seat was never in poor repair for long, the ancestors always took care of it. That is probably the secret of Burg Gnandstein's survival through the centuries as an important work of architecture.

Away from the ancestors, to the castle chapel. A narrow room arched over with star-shaped vaulting. Soft light streams through the coloured side-windows that are set in deep recesses. No fewer than three altars stand in the room. And Jesus of Nazareth is nailed to the Cross. Chapels and churches make people fall silent. What an effect! If only it were always possible. In that case, architects would be gods, and there would be nothing but peacefulness in the world. Nothing in this room is falsified. When the chapel was restored in the late 1960s, the experts largely restored it to its original state. All the glass windows except two are 20th century, but the

The Allies' Room

painting on the gallery balustrade, the floor of Kohren ceramic tiles and the pews date back to around 1500. On the walls, paintings. Christian art has been brought together in the chapel and gallery: paintings and sculptures, books, engravings.

It was Heinrich von Einsiedel who had the chapel built. He was certainly a god-fearing young man, and seemingly one who enjoyed the pleasures of life. He dedicated a winged altar to each of his three wives, to the third during her lifetime. It is not known for certain who made these icons to religious faith. They are probably from a Zwickau workshop. And a great craftsman is said to have lent a hand to the unknown master, the wood-carver Peter Breuer, a pupil of the famous Tilman

1932 The von Einsiedel family opens a local history museum in some rooms of the castle.

1939 The Einsiedels sell the castle and estate to their daughter, Baroness von Friesen.

1945 Expropriation as a result of land reform.

1947 The county museum is opened in Burg Gnandstein.

1968 The chapel is restored.

Since 1991 Works to the inner tower courtyard and archaeological surveys has been carried out.

The Late Gothic chapel

1992 The Free State of Saxony takes over the complex.

1993 Burg Gnandstein becomes a state-owned castle enterprise.

Riemenschneider. The back part of the chapel is devoted to the Reformation. The Einsiedels were among the first noblemen to support Martin Luther. They are known to have asked the Wittenberg Reformer for advice. It is amazing how much artistic sense the Einsiedels possessed, the eye they had for the values of their time. That, too, was the soil in which Saxony grew. In the other rooms, which have a light, congenial air, stories from the Napoleonic days are on show, Baroque furniture, craftsmanship and Theodor Körner, the singer and soldier who fell in battle against Napoleon. Back into the light, to the top of the keep. The Kohrener Land is a gently undulating countryside, villages nestle amid the greenery like

General view from the south-east

a promise. Everything comes from somewhere, lucky are those who know their origins. Burg Gnandstein has a few tales to tell about its own.

About the origin of the von Einsiedel family

In about 830, there lived in Bohemia a Count Berthold von Sulgow. For many years his marriage remained childless. Then, following a vow made by his wife, God finally blessed him with a son, who was baptised Meginrad. Meginrad, as his mother had vowed, dedicated himself to the service of the Lord. He did not enter a monastery, however, but withdrew to a hermitage. At that time, it was not yet compulsory for priests to remain celibate, so he took a wife, according to the words of the Scriptures: »It is not good for man to be alone.« Soon, Meginrad was the happy father of several children. They, too, did not leave their father's residence. Finally, in 1281, one of Meginrad's descendants by the name of Grubo, returned to the world. Instead of the hermit's habit he donned a suit of armour and instead of the rosary he took up the sword. Soon, Grubo made a name for himself in battles and tournaments, all he kept was the name Einsiedel, which was passed on to numerous sons and daughters.

Gräße, J.G. Th.: Der Sagenschatz des Königreichs Sachsen, Dresden, 1974, p. 283 ff.

Burg Kriebstein

Burg Kriebstein reveals some secrets

Burg Kriebstein (Kriebstein Castle) stands hard by the road, surrounded by trees and shimmering light. The writer Joseph Freiherr von Eichendorff would surely make his hero the Taugenichts, or good-for-nothing, pick up his violin and strike up a song to the castle. The first note: the towering Gothic residential tower, the steep slate roofs, the turrets that seem to pull the building upward. And the second: the walls growing out of the rock. Deep below in the valley, lined by green woods, flows the Zschopau, roaring and swirling and foaming as it slips over a weir. Castle and sky are reflected in the dark blue of the river that encloses Burg Kriebstein on three sides.

What would the singer care if one were to puzzle over whether the castle is built on walls dating back to the Romanesque era? True insiders know the answer: despite all the recent excavations and research, no proof has been found. But the castle has stood by the river and the rock has borne the matching stones for more than 600 years. Shades of ochre and brown. The Free State of Saxony's decision to select the castle, along with numerous others, for complete renovation was well-considered. It is regarded as the work of architecture in Saxony that has managed to »keep its (Gothic) character up until the present day.« And the third principal note which Eichendorff would tease out of the violin would be very much in accord with his taste. Outer walls, plastered interior walls and vaults still reveal secrets, make faded colours shimmer.

An unexpected discovery was made in 1986. Researchers and restorers were at work. They uncovered a chimney in the castle and found a treasure, »nine metres of art,« splendid Chinese vases, a porcelain sculpture by Johann Joachim Kaendler, the famous Meißen porcelain designer, beautifully colourful textile collages. »Where did it come from?« they

Page 127:
View from the River Zschopau

Late Gothic wall-paintings in the chapel

1384 First recorded mention of the castle »Krywensteyn« as a lien of Dietrich von Beerwalde; the residential tower was also built around this time.

By 1407 Chapel wing and Gothic hall are completed.

1465 Hugold III von Schleinitz, chief marshall of Elector Ernst and Duke Albrecht, buys the castle and estate of Kriebstein.

1471 The work of Arnold von Westfalen shapes the residential castle's Gothic character. Alterations and extensions to the housekeeping wing, the rear castle, the kitchen building and the well-room.

From 1490 Frequent changes of ownership.

ca. 1500 The coloured trompe l'oeil architectural frame of the treasure vault is made.

1544–1550 The Kriebstein estate experiences its greatest expansion under Georg von Carlowitz.

1549 The Alexius Altar from the secularised monastery of Waldheim is brought to the castle.

From 1561 Further frequent changes of owner, including Elector August (1583).

1665–1689 Under the Schönbergs, lively building activity with an additional storey added to the wing facing the Zschopau and the gatehouse.

1825–1945 The von Arnim family owns the castle and estate.

wondered. The answer was found. The treasure was from Schloss Steinort in East Prussia, the property of the von Lehndorff family. Heinrich Graf von Lehndorff was one of the men involved in the plan to assassinate Hitler on 20 July 1944. The Nazi Volksgerichtshof, or People's Court, sentenced him to death. The Nazis confiscated the works of art and for safe-keeping took them to Burg Kriebstein, which was used to house endangered art during World War II. We owe the preservation of these art treasures to the valet of the Arnim family, which owned Kriebstein until the expropriation of the landowning aristocracy in East Germany. Shortly before the end of the war, he hid the precious objects in the chimney.

1866–1868 Extensive alterations in neo-Gothic style are carried out under the supervision of court architect, Carl Moritz Haenel.

1930 Parts of the castle are opened to the public.

1933 During works to secure the building, wall-paintings are discovered in the castle chapel. They are exposed and restored.

1943–1947 The castle is used as a place of safe-keeping for works of art from Dresden and East Prussia.

1945 Expropriation following the land reform. The castle is used as dwellings and by the forest administration.

1949 The museum is reopened.

1952–1992 Burg Kriebstein is a county museum.

Since 1990 The castle has been the headquarters and office of the Saxony state branch of the Deutsche Burgenvereinigung e.V. (German Castles Association).

1993 Burg Kriebstein becomes a state-owned castle enterprise.

This find is on show in the treasure vault, a fine room. It was none less than the builder of the Albrechtsburg in Meißen, the Late Gothic master Arnold von Westfalen, who left his designer's will in the vaulted room. This room, too, was discovered only recently. Conservationists and restorers searched for years for faded traces and finds they suspected were lurking beneath the layers of plaster. Their aim was clear: every original feature rescued from its hiding place was to be preserved. Beneath numerous layers of paint, they came upon remains of the earliest colours. That made them sure that the room could be restored to its late 15th-century condition. Everything the conservationists discovered was preserved and anything missing was sensitively added. The result was a room in light shades of red. Trompe l'oeil paintings create the illusion of ribbed vaulting. Cheerful, economical decorations beautify the surfaces. As if that were not enough, wall and ceiling paintings dating from the 15th to 17th century came to light.

Another sensation was the discovery of the castle well, which had been filled in at some stage. Masses of rubble were removed. The effort was worthwhile. The excavators discovered many old stonemasons' marks and archaeological finds. The well was probably sunk in the last third of the 15th century. So, step by step, a significant historic monument is being given back to the present.

Art historians regard the Alexius altar as one of Burg Kriebstein's particular gems. Again, we have one man to thank for its preservation. When the Reformation seized nearby Waldheim, the town's Augustinian monastery was dissolved. The last prior saved the altar, which would otherwise certainly have been destroyed, and took it to Kriebstein Castle for safe-keeping. That is how the only altar in Saxony depicting St. Alexius was saved from destruction. It has now been restored and testifies to the skill of the artist who made it in around 1520.

The castle had more than 30 changes of owner. Its proprietors included illustrious families of the Saxon nobility. One Dietrich von Beerwalde inherited the place from his father. The first documentary record of the castle building dates back to 1384. The castle was extended by Hugold III von Schleinitz, a senior official under Elector Ernst and Duke Albrecht, who had broken their vow to rule the Electorate of Saxony jointly from the Albrechtsburg in Meißen. Perhaps Hugold's greatest merit was to have got Arnold von Westfalen to carry out the alterations, for otherwise he is burdened with a serious accusation. Duke Albrecht blamed him for the division of the Saxon territories: for example, »he made me so that my dear brother split with me and thus tore our whole land apart…« Are these the words of a prince who had realised his mistake too late and was trying to clear his name?

The path up to the castle

Inside the castle, a museum has been established. It documents history and the passage of time, furniture stands in its rooms. Ancestors look out from valuable frames. It will take time to finish renovating and restoring the castle. But one thing is certain: it will be done. The roar of the Zschopau breaks the silence of the museum. The rock drops hard and steeply to the river bank. The castle is lucky to have attracted increasing interest. It is to tell future generations about Saxon Late Gothic architecture, about the Saxon nobility's zeal for building. That would be the fourth note that Eichendorff would make his Taugenichts strike up.

The faithful woman of Kriebstein

Schloss Kriebstein, situated in a delightful part of the Zschopau valley, was built (between 1382 and 1407) by a rich nobleman, Dietrich Bärwald or von Bernwalde, who fortified himself in it. Subsequently, on Shrove Tuesday of the year 1415, another nobleman of the Staupitze (von Reichenstein) family attacked him and held the place unlawfully. Margrave Friedrich the Pugnacious then called up the citizens of Freiberg, besieged the castle and violently forced its surrender. The prince allowed the said Staupitze's wife to leave, taking with her anything she wanted and could carry. Thereupon, abandoning her treasures and jewellery, she carried nothing but her husband out of the castle. This act moved the Margrave, notwithstanding the sentence already passed on him, to show mercy and spare her husband's life.

Quoted from Meiche, A.: Sagenburch des Königreichs Sachsen. Leipzig, 1903, p. 801

Schloss Rochlitz

Kings, princes and women at Schloss Rochlitz

It is worth going to Rochlitz for the panorama alone. The palace's twin towers rise in splendid isolation above the Mulde valley, crowned by slate-covered, dark conical roofs. The Fürstenhaus or princes' building, the Querhaus or transverse building and the main castle building rest in the corn-yellow light. The complex reminds one of Romanesque-style weight and massiveness. This appearance does not deceive. Rochlitz's past really does reach back to the beginnings of German history on the Elbe and Mulde. The Liudolfingian Heinrich I had Albrechtsburg (Meißen) built in 929, and the castle in Rochlitz is first mentioned in 995. Like Meißen, Rochlitz was built in an area won from the Western Slavs in battle to safeguard the conquered territory. Admittedly, no more has survived of that time on the Mulde than on the Elbe. Schloss Rochlitz (Rochlitz Palace) was first an imperial castle, then a state castle of the Wettins, property of the Free State of Saxony, and from 1935 it belonged to the German Reich. It has a thousand years of history behind it and maybe an exciting future ahead. The palace is now back in the possession of the Free State of Saxony.

On approaching the castle, the crumbling plaster of the facades becomes visible. Windows are boarded up, walls await restoration. Those who want to can take pleasure in the charm of bygone centuries, romantic transitoriness. Certainly, those responsible for the palace see things differently. They want things to change and the first successes have already been chalked up. One cause for celebration is that the palace chapel has been partially restored. Painted ceilings and walls glow. A cembalo holds the promise of concerts. The former prison, whose buildings disfigured the palace courtyard for nearly a century and a half, has been demolished. At last, the

*Page 133:
The Late Gothic palace chapel: looking up at the »singers' gallery,« with the »dukes' gallery,« to the left and the chancel to the right*

The palace complex with the two towers

995 First mention of the name »Rochlinze.«

1009 The first direct mention of a castle, by Thietmar von Merseburg.

In the 11th century German kings and emperors stay there on several occasions.

1143 The castle passes into Wettin ownership, is the seat of one of the sovereign's stewards and remains a regional administrative headquarters until the 19th century.

1156–1210 As the residence of a branch of the Wettins, the castle experiences its first phase of building: gate-tower, transverse building, pump-room, main castle building, towers.

1286–1291 The later Margrave Friedrich the Bold (der Freidige) resides in Rochlitz, the towers are extended and used as a prison.

1296–1298 The castle temporarily succumbs to the king's occupation forces.

1360–1400 The second building phase occurs under the rule of Wilhelm I (the One-Eyed)'s. Until 1602, the castle is used several times as the residence of the Saxon royal family.

1436–1445 The castle houses the joint Wetting state archive.

1482–1502 The third major building phase takes place under the dowager Duchess Amalia, the palace character is emphasised.

courtyard's original shape is revealed in its proper proportions and the fortifications can be seen. The Fürstenhaus is next in line for renovation. It seems as if Schloss Rochlitz really is heading for better times. The building has long deserved to do so, for there is much here of which Saxon history is made. Art historians stress that Schloss Rochlitz is part of the cultural landscape of the Mulde region. The Late Gothic building phase is significant, they say. The palace was eight times the residence of the Saxon royal house. »The remembrance value is high,« writes one connoisseur.

Remembrance – of what? That kings held court here and issued documents? That the Wettins came by the castle when it was presented to Margrave Konrad of Meißen, and that it subsequently reverted to being an imperial castle for a short time? That Heinrich der Erlauchte resided at Rochlitz from 1251 to 1254? He was a prince with a feeling for art and a Minnesinger. The Heidelberg lieder manuscript proves it. Six of his compositions have been preserved in it. That the castle resisted Hussite attacks? That it was a state prison and administrative headquarters? That Schloss Rochlitz was the residence of several noblewomen?

Several women were closely connected with Schloss Rochlitz. The dowager Duchess Amalia, sister of the brothers Elector Ernst and Duke Albrecht, became a significant builder. She lived in the castle for 20 years, dying in 1502. Under her influence, the building started to be transformed into a palace, though its castle character remained.

The dowager Duchess Elisabeth, sister of Philipp, Landgrave of Hesse, and daughter-in-law of Duke George the Bearded, must have been a courageous woman. Historians believe she tried to prevent the Schmalkaldic War from breaking out – sadly, in vain. She had more success with her veneration of Luther. She introduced the Reformation in the district of

View from the Zwickau Mulde

Rochlitz. That will have greatly displeased George the Bearded, who resisted Luther's doctrine with all his might.

Christiane Eberhardine, the unfortunate wife of Augustus the Strong, had travel apartments in keeping with her status established in the palace. She often stayed at Rochlitz during her annual journeys to spas.

Furthermore, Rochlitz is associated with a Dresden court scandal. Elector Johann Georg IV, brother of Augustus the Strong, had fallen in love with Sibylle von Neitschütz. Nobody could talk him out of his passion. The couple seemed inseparable. He was already married and wanted to take her as his second wife. In the heyday of their love, he gave Sibylle the lovely palace of Pillnitz as a present. A scandal. The elec-

1537–1547 The palace is the residence of dowager Duchess Elisabeth, who introduced the Reformation in the district of Rochlitz. The first Protestant sermon in the palace chapel is delivered in 1537.

1588/89 Thorough building repairs are carried out.

1591–1602 The palace is the residence and dowager dwelling of Electress Sophia.

1618–1648 During the Thirty Years War, a fire breaks out in the lower palace as a result of capture and plundering by Swedish troops.

After 1717 The period of decline and neglect of the buildings sets in.

1852–1961 Schloss Rochlitz is a prison for people awaiting trial.

1892 The museum is founded.

1935 The palace is transferred to the Reich.

1944/45 It is a place of safe-keeping for Saxon archives and museum collections.

1945–1947 Headquarters of the NKWD, the Soviet secret service.

1948 The museum is reopened.

1994 Schloss Rochlitz becomes a state-owned castle enterprise.

1995 1,000-year jubilee celebrations.

The great court kitchen (14th century)

tor's family was beside itself. Schloss Pillnitz in the possession of a whore! Johann Georg went one better. At his instigation, Sibylle received the title »Imperial Countess von Rochlitz.« It is not certain whether she ever entered the palace. Her premature death of smallpox ended the liaison. Johann Georg, who is said to have kissed his beloved on her deathbed in despair, followed her to the grave a few days later. He had caught her smallpox.

Schloss Rochlitz is used as a museum. This began with the opening of an exhibition room in 1893. Hardly anything remains of the castle's former interior furnishings. It is »one of the many Wettin palaces that have been swept clean.« The rooms themselves have long become a museum: the palace

Gravestone in the chapel

chapel, the great court kitchen, the restored Duchess's Parlour, architectural history of the Late Gothic and Renaissance era, the two dungeons and the torture chamber, the light and dark towers, a place for prisoners, the Long Cellar. Much remains to be done in the museum, too. But as we have said, better times for the palace are in sight.

Out of the large palace courtyard to the bridge resting on three arches. What a view! The Mulde flows calmly through the valley. The gently rolling hills vibrate like the playing of a flute. And those who make the effort to climb down the hill to the river will experience the long facade of Rochlitz palace, built by unknown architects, powerful and for eternity.

The ghost on the Sauberg at Rochlitz

Opposite Schloss Rochlitz stands a sizeable hill, the former Weinberg, now known as the Sauberg, whose western part is called the Mützenburg. People say it is haunted by the »white woman of the palace,« driven out of the palace by some sad fate. Others claim to have seen a dog with a »fiery head« roaming about.

One summer night, two Rochlitz soldiers returning through the so-called Heller valley from a dance in Nosswitz, suddenly saw a ghostly, illuminated castle on the Mützenburg. They were exchanging views about the mysterious apparition when a barrel came rolling down the hill. They made to strike it with their sabres, but their arms seemed paralysed, so, frightened, they hastily continued on their way. Another legend says:

Around the middle of the 18th century, there lived in Rochlitz a very rich man who owned various fields and a small piece of forest on the Mützenburg. One fine day he ordered his farm-hand to clear the woodland, but ordered him not to remove a tree stump about one cubit tall in the middle of the wood. The farm-hand obeyed orders. After finishing his work, he thought to himself, »Why should that single stump stay there, I'll chop that one down too.« This he proceeded to do, but afterwards he was paralysed for some considerable time and unable to get up from the ground where he had sat down to rest.

Zimmermann, R.: Sagen und Märchen aus dem Tal der Zwickauer Mulde, Chemnitz, 1901

Burg Scharfenstein

The end of isolation, or the longing for light

Of late, an exciting chapter has been written in the history of mediaeval Scharfenstein Castle, in Scharfenstein on the Zschopau. For decades, the castle was closed to the public. After World War II, it was a training centre and nursery school for the children of miners of Wismut AG. Later, it was a corrective school for difficult boys. Most recently, a workshop for juveniles was housed within its mediaeval walls. To some extent, that suited the buildings. The state felt obliged to keep the castle buildings habitable and prevent the building from falling into decay. Then came the political turnaround. In the third year after German reunification, the workshop was closed. The castle stood above the town shrouded in silence and wind. That was not a good state of affairs. Castles are like other dwellings, if they are not used they quickly deteriorate. The Free State of Saxony made funds available and a plan was drawn up for putting the castle to use. In the meantime, much has been done. People are talking of a Renaissance in Burg Scharfenstein (Scharfenstein Castle). And indeed, there are some amazing things to see.

The Zschopau is unjustifiably overshadowed by the much-lauded Saale and the mighty Elbe. But castles stand proudly and boldly on hills along the banks of the Zschopau, too. Presumably, too few singers sang their praises. But that is another subject, or almost. The point now is to see what there is to discover in Scharfenstein Castle. A narrow, asphalt path leads to an old lime tree, then takes a sharp bend to the left. What a sight! The castle looks like a stage set. The keep in ochre, a Gothic gable, white-washed facades and an intricate Renaissance gate in luminous beauty. The courtyard is not large, it has the look of an old gentleman's parlour. And the keep rises like an outsize sculpture cut out of the bedrock.

Page 141:
View of the castle

The castle and outbuildings

1349/50 First documentary mention in Friedrich the Strict's fief book. The castle is held by Johann von Waldenburg as a margravial fief.

1372 In the Treaty of Pirna, Emperor Charles IV confirms the Margrave of Meißen as owner of Burg Scharfenstein.

1439 The castle is mortgaged to Liborius von Senftleben, master of the Freiberg mint. After that, there were several owners.

1492 Heinrich von Einsiedel buys the castle.

Mid–16th century The complex is thoroughly renovated under Heinrich Abraham von Einsiedel; reception rooms, church and dowager's wing and the gatehouse are built.

1632/33 The castle is plundered twice during the Thirty Years War.

In the 17th century The castle building is completed. The coat-of-arms of the Einsiedel and Ponickau alliance on the south-east portal dates from this period.

1921 The castle suffers extensive fire damage.

1921–1923 The whole complex is rebuilt in its previous form.

1931 The von Einsiedel family possessions are auctioned. The apothecary and pharmaceuticals manufacturer, Fritz Eulitz, buys the castle.

Curiousity arises about the interior, which was completely emptied when the workshop was closed down. Contents had to be found for 55 rooms.

At the entrance to the first storey stands a miner whose arms can be set in motion. They beat a drum, as if to say, roll up, roll up! The bright, colourful world of Erzgebirge crafts receives you. Nutcrackers, incense-burners shaped like human figures, miners, large and small, red and blue and black. Angels of light and trumpeters, pyramids, wooden candelabras, and toys. The first cars, the mail-van, the fire brigade. Nativities, Mary and Joseph, the Three Wise Men, the Christmas Mountain. The folk art that helped the mountain-dwellers to survive when ore and work dried up, is on parade. What variety, what changes in the art of wood-carving since the 19th century! In three years, a completely new museum of Erzgebirge Christmas crafts and toys has come into being, a land for children and grown-ups and aficionados. The longing

1942–1946 The castle serves as a place of safe-keeping for Dresden art treasures.

1945 Expropriation in the wake of land reform, later a nursery school for the children of miners of Wismut AG, a children's home and a juvenile workhouse.

1993 The castle becomes a state-owned castle enterprise and is opened to the public.

1995 Opening of the Erzgebirge Christmas and Toy Museum. Manufacture and sale of Erzgebirge crafts.

for the light, the miners' hope of returning to the surface as they descended into the darkness of the shafts, is expressed in allegorical picture-language in these rooms. It is the longing to live a life fit for human beings in the barren mountains. And this leitmotif gives the exhibition meaning and direction. It is amazing to see what the castle has kept from being forgotten and lost, and how the senses are stimulated. Notes and sounds in the rooms, humming and whirring, sounds of sawing and carving. Wood-carvers can be seen at work on television screens, accompanied by quiet Christmas carols in the middle of summer. The museum experts aim to seduce, to make people dream. Gingerbread and Christmas lights and walnuts. You can even crack them. A sack full of walnuts stands there with nutcrackers at the ready.

Saxony has a new museum and Burg Scharfenstein a future. Some luck was involved in making this exhibition possible. Johannes Martin of Hamburg, a passionate collector and former resident of Leipzig, had been collecting Erzgebirge woodcarvings for decades because he liked them and feared that they might be lost. He has made them available to Burg Scharfenstein on permanent loan. What a stroke of providence: the collector sees his treasures in a worthy setting, and allows them to return to the region whence they came.

The castle administrators have further plans. Renovation of the buildings is to be completed within the next few years. Then additional rooms in the dowager's wing will be placed at the museum's disposal. By then, the museum will be prepared. The experts plan to document the life of Erzgebirge poachers, and tell the story of a legendary figure, Karl Stülpner. The fact that he was born in Scharfenstein heightens the challenge of drawing a fair picture of this man who was so often denigrated by the authorities. In addition, more attention will be given to the Einsiedel family, which was largely responsible

»Longing for light« exhibition

for giving the castle its present appearance. Thus, Burg Scharfenstein will cast light on another piece of the history of the state of Saxony. One can leave the castle at ease. It has been released from its isolation and the Zschopau valley has gained a further attraction.

How Karl Stülpner drove out the Cossacks

In 1813, the Austrians marched to Saxony to fight Napoleon, only to be defeated and taken prisoner again by him at Dresden. Shortly afterwards, a general amnesty was declared, Stülpner returned with his men to Scharfenstein and six weeks later was finally discharged.

In the same year, as all the residents of our Erzgebirge know only too well from sad experience, a large number of Cossacks roamed through the countryside throughout the late autumn. They sought out every hiding-place like bloodhounds, often behaving in a very robber-like manner. So it came to pass that one day about 200 men, so-called farmer Cossacks, came to Scharfenstein, plundered it and took away everything they could carry. Even Stülpner was not spared: all his belongings and those of his family were forcibly carried off by the rabble. Indignant at this impertinence, Stülpner hurried after two stragglers and, after dealing them several hard blows in the ribs, threw them into the Zschopau to give them a Russian steam bath.

Shortly afterwards, with the help of a Hungarian corporal who was posted in Schloss Scharfenstein as a guard, Stülpner liberated the village of Griessbach, which was being plundered by a crowd of Cossacks, from the robbers. His long acknowledged daring and bravery had won him such a reputation that everywhere in the area where such plundering was carried out, people called on him to help. His presence of mind and strong fists prevented many a case of maltreatment of the poor inhabitants, and their property from being snatched.

Schönberg, C. H. W. (ed.): Carl Stülpner's merkwürdiges Leben und Abenteuer als Wildschütz … Zschopau, 1835, p. 121 f.

Schloss Augustusburg

Augustusburg – Crown of the Erzgebirge

Augustusburg lies not far from Chemnitz, above the Zschopau valley. Old beeches frame the gigantic quadrangular palace complex and the former stables and farm buildings. It is one of the largest stately homes in Saxony. And the palace chapel houses a true gem, a painting by Lucas Cranach the Younger. Anyone looking from its hill across the undulating countryside comes to the conclusion that a superb location was chosen for the palace.

Augustusburg ranks among the Saxon palace museums. It presents itself in a variety of exhibition rooms, and has done so for a long time. Motor-cycle enthusiasts will find plenty to see. And those who feel like returning to the mode of travel of bygone centuries can imagine themselves stepping into one of the many carriages, or boarding a sleigh. Guaranteed, travelling in one of these high-wheeled carriages, though some were solidly furnished and upholstered, was certainly not all pleasure. The palace also has something to offer nature-lovers. In the Hasenhaus or hares' house, stuffed animals and birds of the Erzgebirge region have been assembled in a replica of their native habitat.

A look into the past explains the choice of location. Before the new Renaissance-style palace was built, a castle stood on the site. Situated in the imperial territory of Pleißenland, it was used for defensive purposes. Those who feel like it can climb to the top of the porphyry summit and feel a shiver of fear. Nothing remained of this first castle, the Schellenberg. A storm of the kind that is said to happen only once in a century nearly blew it away. Lightning destroyed the remains. For about 20 years, the ruins and stones lay untouched. Then Elector August I discovered the place. He was in a hurry to build a new hunting lodge and summer palace. That project

Page 147:
Altar and chancel in the palace church

The Renaissance castle complex

1206 First mention of the manor of Schellenburg.

1324 As a result of the Schellenberg Feud, the manor passes to the Wettins.

1568–1572 Burg Schellenberg, partly destroyed by fire, is demolished and, under Elector August, the Augustusburg is built by the architects Hieronymus Lotter and Count Rochus von Lynar. The wall-paintings are by Heinrich Göding.

1572 The church (designed by Erhardt van der Meer) with an altar painting by Lucas Cranach the Younger, is consecrated. Until 1845 it is the village's principal church.

Until 1611 Schloss Augustusburg is used as a hunting lodge for the Elector's court.

1632/33 Swedish troops occupy and plunder the palace.

1676–1681 A garrison is housed there.

After 1694 The trophies and some of the palace contents are transferred to Moritzburg and Hubertusburg. The palace is seldom used.

1756–1763 Damage is sustained during the Seven Years War.

After 1763 The palace is used for various purposes, including district headquarters, court, prison, store, military hospital (1813).

1798–1802 The palace complex is altered according to plans by Christian Traugott Weinlig.

didn't turn out well, either for him or the architect. It ended in arguments and hatred.

In 1567 the Elector ordered the citizens of the town, which was then called Schellenberg, to remove the ruins from the hill. He was determined to celebrate his victory over his rival, the Ernestine Johann Friedrich and his ally Grumbach, by erecting a major building. August had certainly learned something from his predecessor, Elector Moritz, who had enhanced his electoral standing and newly acquired abundance of power by undertaking alterations to the Dresden Schloss. The decision was swiftly taken, but Elector August still needed an architect. He wanted someone of supreme building ability. Finally, he decided on Hieronymus Lotter, mayor of Leipzig and and creator of the city's Altes Rathaus, or Old Town Hall.

Lotter hesitated. He was no longer young. As an experienced man, he suspected that working for his ruler would be difficult. Perhaps he already knew about the Elector's obstinacy and miserliness. He tried to get out of it by citing his age, 69. August and his wife Anna pressed Lotter, formally requested him, and promised to »commemorate his work with particular favour.« Citizen Lotter allowed himself to be persuaded after the Elector had agreed not to interfere in the building works. Hieronymous Lotter was to regret it.

Building started in September 1568. The remains of Schellenberg castle were demolished. Soon, delays occurred in the building works. The Elector kept urging, but Lotter resisted. He wanted to build a decent summer palace and hunting lodge. The bricklayers and carpenters were grumbling that they were being driven too hard. They demanded more money, even laid down their tools. Lotter, who in the meantime had fallen ill, was given an assistant. He, however, only wanted to do his own thing and submitted his own proposals

State coach in the horse-drawn carriages museum

for the palace building to the Elector. In short, the relationship between the client and Lotter deteriorated rapidly to the point where it was intolerable.

The Elector accused the aged Lotter of not paying sufficient attention to Augustusburg, of deliberately delaying the building works to extract more money. When the ruler started refusing payments, leaving bills unpaid, Lotter paid from his own pocket. Finally, shortly before the palace was completed, the Elector appointed someone else to supervise the works. And when the time came for the official opening, he did not even deem it necessary to invite Lotter. Indeed, shortly afterwards he banned him from entering the castle. Nor did Lotter subsequently receive any gratitude. August remained

Since 1831 The palace has been owned by the state of Saxony and used by public authorities.

After 1918 The Erzgebirgs-museum, a restaurant and a youth hostel are established.

1933–1945 Schloss Augustusburg is a school for Nazi regional leaders (Gauführer) and military fitness training camp, a place of safe-keeping for works of art, provisional accommodation for refugees.

1951 Opening of the local history museum.

1960 The two-stroke motor-cycle museum is opened in the kitchen building.

1969 A game and ornithology museum is established in the Hasenhaus.

1989 Opening of the viewing tower with gallery in the Lindenhaus.

1991 The collection of horse-drawn coaches in the stable building becomes an independent museum.

1993 Schloss Augustusburg becomes a state-owned castle enterprise. The Adlerhof (eagle courtyard) and the Falkenhof (falcon courtyard) are laid out.

1997 An exhibition on hunting and farming is opened.

Trompe l'oeil painting in the Hasensaal

15,000 florins in his debt. The once so respected and wealthy mayor of Leipzig died a pauper. That was the Elector's gratitude. Nonetheless, the proud Lotter was not going to let his work be denied. He wrote to his lord: »And I thank God in heaven that I took such a building without defects, right to the end.«

Schloss Augustusburg, despite its plainness, was soon known far beyond the Saxon borders. Thomas Corneille, a brother of the famous French dramatist, described it thus: »The quadrangular building is relatively plain. But the portals are magnificent, the four towers dominant (they no longer exist). Between them lie the side-wings.« In over 400 years the palace has undergone many changes. It is a great pity about the corner buildings, which used to be one storey taller. The original interior decor was lost, too. But the Renaissance proportions, the clearly structured wings, the impressive courtyards, the portals and the room structure, remain.

In the motor-cycle museum

After Elector August, the Wettin rulers took less and less interest in the Augustusburg. Only rarely was it used for hunting or festivities. It was a prison and a prisoner-of-war camp. August the Strong even had 330 sets of antlers taken to his new hunting palace, the Hubertusburg in Wermsdorf, and Schloss Moritzburg. The palace went through hard times, until it finally became state property and, later, a museum.

In recent decades, the building has been renovated and restored and has recently attracted further attention. The administrators came up with a new idea and an exhibition on hunting and farming was opened. In future, too, Augustusburg will remain true to is tradition of being a palace with many museums.

Prince Lieschen

One hot July day, the chancellor's coach came rushing into the entrance of the Dresden Schloss. People were so nonplussed that they didn't even have time for a greeting. The ponderers among them started sniffing around as if there were a smell of fire and war.

Hardly had the palace guard lined up than His Excellency von Pflug had dashed past them. The discussion with His Majesty took place behind closed doors and the to-ing and fro-ing broke the pure stillness of the early morning.

»The devil take him, Pflug, if that's right,« the King said at last. Then, in person, he wrote a brief order. Ten minutes later a lieutenant with twelve hussars raced out of the gate, galloping hard through the streets of Dresden toward Schloss Augustusburg.

»It could still be a mistake, Majesty,« Herr von Pflug hastened to say. »His Royal Majesty Electoral Prince August, according to my information, is alive and well in Vienna.«

But in Augustusburg Park, drums and trumpets were sounding. Travellers were loafing around the closed railings. The sky was blue, the sun yellow, and the highway shimmered with white dust.

That was some fellow, the Electoral Prince! His father sent him to Vienna, and the son disguised himself as a scholar and returned to Saxony as quickly and secretly as possible. He wanted to check up on things without being recognised. But was he a man at all? For three weeks now, he had been living in the palace of Herr von Günther, the chief fish-keeper and steward of Augustusburg. There were firework displays and hunts. And day after day the carriages of the nobility rolled from all around toward Schloss Augustusburg.

Then, in the midst of the Augustusburgers' evviva cries, came the hoarse command of the lieutenant from Dresden: »Dismount!« A servant ran to tell the master of the house. But the lieutenant only drew a crumpled piece of paper out of his dusty jacket, a curt greeting, a short bow, and with that two hussars had seized His Royal Majesty the Electoral Prince and the chief fish-keeper under the arms. Another command, a short about-turn, a rearing of horses, then the whole procession disappeared in a cloud of dust.

His Majesty the King was still laughing long after he had gone to his royal bed on the evening of this grim day.

He laughed so hard that the red plush canopy with its white ostrich feathers was bouncing up and down. And on the edge of the royal bed sat Herr von Pflug, who was laughing too.

»We'll call her Prince Lieschen, Pflug. And we'll make Günther the court jester!«

Next day, the whole royal capital of Dresden was laughing, and many knew that His Royal Highness from Augustusburg had turned out to be – a girl. As the daughter of a master clothmaker from Wolkenstein in the Erzgebirge, who was feeling restless, she had dressed in men's clothing and secretly run away from her father. Herr von Günther, taking her for the real Electoral Prince, had invited all the nobility, and had even starting thinking of himself as the future Chancellor.

Prince Lieschen lived a long time, though in well-behaved captivity. She only ever wore men's clothes, and for the rest of his life Herr von Günther had to give her one imperial taler every day for her keep.

Quoted from Zerkaulen, H.: Prinz Lieschen. In: Miniaturen in Weiß und Grün, Dresden 1936, p. 130 ff.

Select bibliography

Barockschloss Rammenau. Dresden, 1993.

Baumbach, Udo: Schloß Rochlitz. Ein Führer durch Burg, Museum und Geschichte. Beucha, 1995.

Burg Mildenstein Leisnig. Schnell, Kunstführer No. 1952. Munich, Zürich, 1992.

Burg Scharfenstein, published by the Saxon Castles Administration. Munich, Berlin, 1995.

Burg Stolpen. Ein heimatkundliches Heft zum Besuch der Burg Stolpen. Published by the Stolpen town council/castle administration. 3rd edition, Dresden, 1984.

Burgen, Schlösser, Gutshäuser in Sachsen. Published by Bruno J. Sobotka in Witten, 1996.

Delau, Reinhard & Pellmann, Udo: Dresden. Halle, 1992.

Ehemaliges Zisterzienserkloster Altzella. Schnell, Kunstführer No. 2048. Munich, Zürich, 1992.

Ermisch, Hubert Georg: Der Zwinger zu Dresden. Berlin, 1952,

Festung Dresden. Published by Staatlich Schlösser und Gärten Dresden. Dresden, 1994.

Geschichte Sachsens. Published by Karl Czok. Weimar, 1989.

Handbuch der historischen Stätten Deutschlands; Sachsen. Published by Walter Schlesinger. Stuttgart, 1990.

Hartmann, Hans-Günther: Pillnitz, Schloß, Park und Dorf. Weimar, 1981.

Hempel, Eberhard: Der Zwinger zu Dresden. Leipzig, 1964.

Löffler, Fritz: Das alte Dresden. Geschichte seiner Bauten. 13th edition, Leizig, 1997.

Magirius, Heinrich: Zur Enstehungsgeschichte des Schlosses Pillnitz und seiner Fassadenbemalung. In: Denkmale in Sachsen. Schriften zur Denkmalpflege in der DDR. Weimar, 1979.

Mrusek, Hans-Joachim: Meißen. Leipzig, 1991.

Naumann, Günther: Sächsische Geschichte in Daten. Berlin, Leipzig, 1991.

Piltz, Georg: Kunstführer durch die DDR. 9th edition. Leipzig, Jena, Berlin, 1969.

Pohl, Hans-Jürgen: Meißen Tourist. Stadführer. Meißen, 1983.

Schloß Weesenstein. Published by the Schloßverwaltung Weesenstein. Dresden, 1994.

Um Stolpen und Neustadt. Werte unserer Heimat. Vol. 17. Berlin, 1970.

Picture credits

Boswank, Herbert, Dresden: p. 45, 49, 51, 53, 54, 62, 70, 72, 73, 77, 80, 81 (top), 83, 85, 96, 107, 127, 133, 135, 137, 138, 139;

Deutsche Luftbild, W. Seelmann & Co. GmbH, Hamburg: p. 61;

Foto Krüger, Nossen: p. 99, 105;

Foto Steiger, Augustusburg: p. 153;

Foto Weber, Augustusburg: p. 147;

Hanke, Gabriele, Dresden: p. 13, 21, 39, 75;

Heli-Veit, Flöha: p. 143;

Karpinski, Jürgen, Dresden: frontispiece, p. 87;

Krull, Dieter und Evelyn, Dresden: p. 12, 91, 93;

Lichtbild-Hempel, Chemnitz: p. 145;

Lieberknecht, Werner, Dresden: p. 18;

Pellmann, Udo, Dresden: p. 7, 15, 17, 29, 95;

Pohle, Christa, Heidenau: p. 67;

Schieckel, Klaus, Stolpen: p. 56;

Schöner, Bettina, Dresden: p. 40;

Schöner, Jörg, Dresden: p. 10, 25, 32, 37, 43, 46, 88, 89, 111, 113, 116, 119, 121, 123, 124, 129, 131, 149, 151, 152;

Staatliche Kunstsammlung Dresden, Gemäldegalerie Neue Meister: p. 81 (bottom);

Thieme, Wolfgang, Chemnitz: p. 141;

Verlagsarchiv: p. 9;

Weber, Gerhard, Grimma: p. 125;

Weber, Klaus-Dieter, Pirna: p. 27, 35;

Walther, Bernd, Heidenau: p. 59, 64, 65;

The pictures on pages 31, 48, 69, 79, 101, 102, 106 and 108 were provided by the respective castle enterprises.

Staatliche Schlösser, Burgen und Gärten Sachsen

Stauffenbergallee 2, 01099 Dresden
Phone +49 (351) 8 27 46 32
Fax +49 (351) 8 27 46 02
Internet: www.schloesser.sachsen.de

1 Dresdner Zwinger, **2** Stallhof, **3** Brühlsche Terrasse/Kasematten
Postal address 1–3:
Staatliche Schlösser und Gärten Dresden
Brühlsche Terrasse/Zwinger/Stallhof
Zwinger/Theaterplatz, 01067 Dresden
Phone +49 (351) 4 91 46 01
Fax +49 (351) 4 91 46 25
Internet: www.schloesser-dresden.de

4 Großer Garten
Staatliche Schlösser und Gärten Dresden
Großer Garten
Kavaliershaus G, Hauptallee 5,
01219 Dresden
Phone +49 (351) 4 45 66 00
Fax +49 (351) 4 45 67 22
Internet: www.schloesser-dresden.de

5 Schloss und Park Pillnitz
Staatliche Schlösser und Gärten Dresden
Schloss Pillnitz
Fliederhof/Kapellenflügel, 01326 Dresden
Phone +49 (351) 2 61 32 60
Fax +49 (351) 2 61 32 80
Internet: www.schloesser-dresden.de
1–5: (follow the signs in Dresden, local public transportation, Elbe streamer)

6 Barockschloss Rammenau
Am Schloß 4, 01877 Rammenau
Phone +49 (35 94) 70 35 59
Fax +49 (35 94) 70 59 83
Internet: www.barockschloss-rammenau.com
A 4 Dresden–Bautzen (exit Burkau);
B 6 Dresden–Bischofswerde–Bautzen (from Bischofswerda towards the freeway)

7 Burg Stolpen
Schloßstraße 10, 01833 Stolpen
Phone +49 (3 59 73) 2 34 10
Fax +49 (3 59 73) 2 34 19
Internet: www.burg-stolpen.de
B 6 Dresden–Bischofswerda (from the B 6 follow the signs)

8 Festung Königstein
01824 Königstein
Phone +49 (3 50 21) 6 46 07
Fax +49 (3 50 21) 6 46 09
Internet: www.festung-koenigstein.de
B 172 Dresden–Königstein–Schmilka; suburban train Dresden–Königstein–Schöna; Elbe streamer

9 Barockgarten Großsedlitz
Parkstraße 85, 01809 Heidenau
Phone +49 (35 29) 5 63 90
Fax +49 (35 29) 56 39 99
Internet: www.barockgarten-grosssedlitz.de
B 172 Dresden–Pirna (follow the signs in Heidenau); suburban train Dresden–Heidenau/Großsedlitz–Schöna

10 Schloss Weesenstein
Am Schloßberg 1, 01809 Müglitztal
Phone +49 (3 50 27) 6 26 29
Fax +49 (3 50 27) 6 26 28
Internet: www.schloss-weesenstein.de
B 172 Dresden–Pirna (in Heidenau towards Altenberg); suburban train Dresden–Schöna (in Heidenau-Nord transfer towards Altenberg)

11 Schloss Moritzburg
01468 Moritzburg
Phone +49 (3 52 07) 87 30
Fax +49 (3 52 07) 8 73 11
Internet: www.schloss-moritzburg.de
A 4 Dresden–Bautzen (exit Dresden–Wilder Mann); A 13 Berlin–Dresden (exit Radeburg) then follow the signs; narrow-gauge railway Radebeul–Radeburg

12 Albrechtsburg Meissen
Domplatz 1, 01662 Meißen
Phone +49 (35 21) 4 70 70,
Fax: +49 (35 21) 47 07 11
Internet: www.albrechtsburg-meissen.de
A 4 Dresden–Autobahndreieck Nossen (exit Wilsdruff, then follow the signs); B 6 Dresden–Meißen–Leipzig; B 101 Freiberg–Meißen–Großenhain; suburban train Dresden–Meißen, Elbe streamer

13 Schloss Nossen
14 Klosterpark Altzella
01683 Nossen
Phone +49 (3 52 42) 5 04 30
Fax +49 (3 52 42) 5 04 33
Internet: www.schloss-nossen.de
www.kloster-altzella.de
A 4 Dresden–Nossen–Chemnitz;
A 14 Dresden–Nossen–Leipzig;
train: Dresden–Meißen– Nossen–Leipzig

15 Burg Mildenstein
Burglehn 6, 04703 Leisnig
Phone +49 (3 43 21) 1 26 52
Fax: +49 (3 43 21) 5 15 37
Internet: www.burg-mildenstein.de
A 14 Dresden–Leipzig (exit Leisnig);
train: Leipzig–Leisnig–Nossen

16 Burg Gnandstein
Burgstraße 3, 04655 Kohren-Sahlis
Phone +49 (3 43 44) 6 13 09
Fax +49 (3 43 44) 6 13 83
B 7 Rochlitz–Altenburg; B 95 Leipzig– Frohburg (follow the signs from there) – Chemnitz

17 Burg Kriebstein
09648 Kriebstein
Phone +49 (3 43 27) 95 20
Fax: +49 (3 43 27) 9 52 22
Internet: www.burg-kriebstein.de
A 4 Chemnitz–Dresden; (exit Chemnitz-Ost, towards Döbeln); A 14 Leipzig–Dresden (exit Döbeln-Nord, towards Mittweida); train: Berlin–Chemnitz, Waldheim Stop

18 Schloss Rochlitz
Sörnziger Weg 1, 09306 Rochlitz
Phone +49 (37 37) 49 23 10
Fax +49 (37 37) 49 23 12
Internet: www.schloss-rochlitz.de
A 14 Leipzig–Dresden (exit Döbeln-Nord, follow B 169 and B 175 towards Zwickau); A 4 Gera–Chemnitz–Dresden (exit Glösa, follow B 107 towards Wurzen)

19 Burg Scharfenstein
Schloßberg 1, 09435 Scharfenstein
Phone +49 (37 25) 7 07 20
Fax +49 (37 25) 70 72 50
Internet: www.die-sehenswerten-drei.de
B 174 Chemnitz–Zschopau (follow the signs) – Marienberg; B 101 Freiberg–Annaberg–Buchholz (follow the signs);
train: Chemnitz–Annaberg

20 Schloss Augustusburg
09573 Augustusburg
Phone +49 (3 72 91) 38 00
Fax +49 (3 72 91) 3 80 24
Internet: www.die-sehenswerten-drei.de
A 4 Chemnitz–Dresden (exit Frankenberg via Flöha); A 72 Chemnitz–Plauen (exit Chemnitz-Süd); B 180 Frankenberg–Zschopau; train: Chemnitz–Erdmannsdorf

21 Schloss und Park Lichtenwalde
Schlossallee 1, 09577 Lichtenwalde
Phone +49 (3 72 06) 8 93 58
Fax +49 (3 72 06) 8 93 60
Internet: www.die-sehenswerten-drei.de
A 4 Chemnitz–Dresden (exit Chemnitz-Ost); B 169 Chemnitz–Frankenberg; 8 km distance from the town centre

22 Schloss Colditz
Schlossgasse 1, 04680 Colditz
Phone +49 (3 43 81) 4 37 77
Fax +49 (3 43 81) 4 37 77
Internet: www.schloss-colditz.de
A14 Dresden–Leipzig (exit Grimma) follow B 107 forward Colditz

Key

to the adjacent map
of the finest palaces,
castles and gardens
in the Free State of Saxony

1 Dresden Zwinger
2 Royal Mews in Dresden
3 Brühl Terrace in Dresden
4 Great Garden in Dresden
5 Pillnitz Palace and Park
6 Rammenau Baroque Palace
7 Stolpen Castle
8 Königstein Fortress
9 Großsedlitz Baroque Garden
10 Weesenstein Palace
11 Moritzburg Palace
12 Albrechtsburg Meissen
13 Nossen Palace
14 Altzella Monastery Park
15 Mildenstein Castle
16 Gnandstein Castle
17 Kriebstein Castle
18 Rochlitz Palace
19 Scharfenstein Castle
20 Augustusburg Palace
21 Lichtenwalde Palace and Park
22 Colditz Palace

Free State of Saxony
Republic of Poland
Brandenburg
Saxony-Anhalt
Free State of Thuringia
Free State of Bavaria
Czech Republik
Torgau
Weißwasser
Hoyerswerda
Leipzig
Riesa
Meißen
Radebeul
Dresden
Bautzen
Görlitz
Löbau
Freital
Pirna
Zittau
Freiberg
Meerane
Chemnitz
Crimmitschau
Glauchau
Zwickau
Aue
Plauen
14
13
4
72
1
2
3
4
5
6
7
8
9
10
11
12
13
14
15
16
17
18
19
20
21
22